Oedipus and the Sphinx

The Threshold Myth
from Sophocles through Freud
to Cocteau

Oedipus
and the Sphinx

ALMUT-BARBARA RENGER

Translation by Duncan Alexander Smart
and David Rice, with John T. Hamilton

University of Chicago Press
Chicago and London

Almut-Barbara Renger is professor of ancient religion and culture and their reception history at the Institute for the Scientific Study of Religion at the Freie Universität Berlin.

The University of Chicago Press, Chicago 60637
The University of Chicago Press, Ltd., London
© 2013 by The University of Chicago
All rights reserved. Published 2013.
Printed in the United States of America

22 21 20 19 18 17 16 15 14 13   1 2 3 4 5

ISBN-13: 978-0-226-04808-6 (cloth)
ISBN-13: 978-0-226-04811-6 (e-book)

This book contains part of the author's habilitation thesis at Goethe University Frankfurt (2009).

Library of Congress Cataloging-in-Publication Data

Renger, Almut-Barbara, author.
    Oedipus and the Sphinx : the threshold myth from Sophocles through Freud to Cocteau / Almut-Barbara Renger ; translation by Duncan Alexander Smart and David Rice, with John T. Hamilton.
        pages ; cm
    Includes bibliographical references and index.
    ISBN 978-0-226-04808-6 (cloth : alkaline paper) — ISBN 978-0-226-04811-6 (e-book) 1. Oedipus (Greek mythology) 2. Sphinxes (Mythology) 3. Sophocles. Oedipus Rex. 4. Oedipus (Greek mythology) in literature. 5. Sphinxes (Mythology) in literature. 6. Mythology, Greek—Appreciation. 7. Freud, Sigmund, 1856–1939—Knowledge—Mythology. 8. Cocteau, Jean, 1889–1963— Knowledge—Mythology. I. Smart, Duncan, translator. II. Hamilton, John T., translator. III. Rice, David G. (David Gerard), 1945–, translator. IV. Title.
BL820.O43R46 2013
809'.93351—dc23

2013000531

♾ This paper meets the requirements of ANSI/NISO Z39.48–1992 (Permanence of Paper).

CONTENTS

⁀ℓℓ

INTRODUCTION

"Cocteau is probably one of the greatest mythographers that the earth has ever borne, if by 'mythographer' one understands: 'he who writes after myths' and 'he who writes myths.'"[1] So said the critic Milorad in 1971, articulating a distinct attribute of Jean Cocteau's creative legacy. Since the beginning of his intensified engagement with antiquity in the 1920s, Cocteau had been collecting stories about the Greco-Roman gods and heroes, rewriting and reworking them according to his own understanding and approach, which was, in the broadest sense of the word, *mythographic*. In service to this pursuit, Cocteau employed several specifically modern techniques, such as montage, collage, and bricolage. He culled and used particular elements from antiquity's mythological storehouse, acting as a *mythographe déconstructeur*, through the recombination and blending together of biblical as well as French and German figures, incorporating traditional, national material as well as elements of the modern, techno-industrial world, all of which subverted the classical role of antiquity as a stable narrative substance.[2] As Cocteau went about this work, two figures inspired him in a particularly enduring way: Orpheus, the singer who bewitched gods, humans, and even animals, plants, and stones with his songs and lyre playing, and went down into the underworld for the sake of his love,

Eurydice; and Oedipus, the king of Thebes, who unwittingly broke two taboos when he killed his father and married his mother.

This study centers on Oedipus—above all, on a specific event in the larger myth cycle: the hero's confrontation with the Sphinx. This scourge of Thebes, who since ancient times had been described as a winged woman with a lion's body, has been consistently affiliated with the hero. Both figures—Oedipus and the Sphinx, as a constellation—have been transmitted in manifold ways from antiquity to modernity, especially from the Renaissance to the twentieth century.[3] To understand how the figure of Oedipus has been received and understood throughout, it is crucial to begin by noting that Aristotle, in the *Poetics*, declared that Sophocles' *Oedipus the King* (Οἰδίπους τύραννος; 429/425 BCE) was the paradigm for the genre of tragedy, especially in terms of plot, the reversal from fortune to misfortune (*peripeteia*), as well as the turn from blinding to self-recognition (*anagnorisis, anagnorismos*).[4] This judgment contributed considerably to the prominence of the Oedipus figure not only in literature, music, the plastic arts, and film, but also in philosophy, literary theory, psychoanalysis, and the human sciences.[5] Elevated to the normative standard of the tragic genre, *Oedipus the King* remains Sophocles' masterpiece. And just as the Oedipus myth constituted a benchmark in antiquity, so does it function in modern thought, thanks to its appropriation by Sigmund Freud. Freud's theory of the Oedipus complex, which he developed through an examination of *Oedipus the King,* has, like Sophocles' tragic representation in antiquity, far outpaced all other modern interpretations and reinterpretations of the tragedy in terms of sheer, broad impact.

Cocteau's engagement with Oedipus is also determined by this broad impact. The Oedipus figure enjoyed conspicuous dispersion across the widely branching oeuvre of this multimedia artist, a dispersion that is traceable not least to his involvement with Sophocles and Freud. Cocteau concerned himself with Oedipus again and again throughout the 1920s, and, in line with his "esthétique du minimum," created numerous "contractions"—abridged stage plays based on works by ancient tragic authors.[6] Following *Antigone* (1922) came *Œdipe-Roi* (1925), begun in 1921–1922 with the subtitle *Adaptation libre d'après Sophocle*, then the libretto for Igor Stravinsky's opera-oratorio

Oedipus Rex (1928), probably written in 1925–1926, which was rendered into Latin by the Jesuit Jean Daniélou,[7] and finally yet another original theatrical piece on the same theme: *La machine infernale*, completed in 1932. In connection with this last work, Cocteau issued explicit statements on Sophocles as well as Freud in the *Journal d'un inconnu*.[8] These statements elucidate how Cocteau's Œdipe is part of a complex network of cross-references and intertextual relations, a system that would be worthwhile to investigate in detail and in greater depth. Admittedly, this study does not aspire to such thoroughness. Instead, *La machine infernale* has been selected as an example of Cocteau's *poésie* (the term he used for all of his work), in order to derive criteria for assessing the significance of this intertextual cluster. As the last of his Oedipus plays, *La machine infernale* remains without question the most important and original in all of Cocteau's work, both for its innovative manner and method, and for the way it weaves Oedipus' "encounter" with the Sphinx into a larger fabric.[9] Although represented since the nineteenth century in literature and the plastic arts as a man-threatening being, unconquerable and unknowable, in Cocteau, the Sphinx is by no means conceived in strictly negative terms. As traditionally characterized, she perversely deviates from the norms of physical and unambiguously human integrity, veering into monstrosity. Such a characterization prevails as a consequence of a Christian and modern concept of subjectivity, which seeks to reinforce human distance from the bestial.[10] In Cocteau, the Sphinx's aberrant qualities have to do, rather, as they did in Egyptian mythology straight into the Greek tradition, with *extraordinary godliness*: as markers of immortality.[11] Cocteau's Sphinx is simultaneously a mortal seventeen-year-old and the immortal goddess Nemesis.

This study, in its first part, will consider the ancient myth of Oedipus: his ancestry, particular ancient traditions, and later reflections. We will pay particular attention to evidence from the fifth century BCE, namely Sophocles' *Oedipus the King*—the tragedy of a highly vaunted "chief among his people," who, as the Chorus concludes, "plummeted down terribly, deep into the ground of misery"—and Oedipus' encounter with the Sphinx, as it was frequently represented in the vase painting of the day. Our primary focus centers on this encounter as the central event in Oedipus' life, one marked by liminality, uncertainty, and ambiguity. The liminal nature of the encounter itself is elaborated as well as the liminality of the Sphinx, one of the most prominent figures of otherness among the multitude scattered across Greek mythology. Figures will describe and evoke what is disparate, disquieting, lawless, or simply outside a given social order. Furthermore, we shall see that even the hero's fate, at every nodal point, is determined by liminality—by a no-longer and a not-yet—and that the entire course of his life, from the moment of being cast out as a child to the final moment in which he casts himself out of Thebes as a freshly blinded king, is a kind of deferred, painful process of self-realization, concluding with the acceptance of what is irresolvably liminal within himself.

To qualify this liminality or threshold state more precisely, I examine the pertinent research of two of the most significant threshold theorists of the twentieth century, Arnold van Gennep and Victor Turner, who postulate that the threshold is not only a place but also a process, exhibiting therefore both a spatial and a temporal dimension. By titling his 1967 investigation "Betwixt and Between," Turner gave an apposite tag to the "threshold phase" in which people find themselves when they have broken free from a particular set of social relationships but have not yet attained admission to the brand-new state they have been approaching. When Oedipus comes before the Sphinx, he finds himself in just such a liminal state, marked by a lack of fixed meaning, by uncertainty and ambiguity. His passage through her zone sunders his past from a future closed off from view. This movement unleashes a dynamic that determines the nature of the oppositions running against each other inside him (foreigner/citizen of Thebes; solver of riddles/a riddle himself; savior of the city/cause of the city's damnation). As Jean-Pierre Vernant puts it in his essay "Ambiguity and Reversal," he is recognizably a creature struck from the same mold as the ambiguous Sphinx herself.

The study's second part focuses on Freud's and Cocteau's analyses of Sophocles' *Oedipus* and thereby deals with two of the twentieth century's most significant reworkings and recontextualizations of the myth. To this end, attention is drawn first of all to Freud—and, of course, to Oedipus as the namesake of one of psychoanalysis' defining theoretical complexes—so as to elucidate the degree to which Cocteau saw in Freud an approach opposite to his own art and artistic concepts. Cocteau did not want to see the fact that Freud's analytical work served to resolve pathological complexes. Rather, he perceived the Viennese professor as an adversary, as a thinker who stood against all the aspects and compositional problems that touched on his work as a *poète*—as a poet, a visual artist, and a filmmaker. As opposed to Freud, Cocteau saw himself as what he de facto was: someone who blurred boundaries and crossed borders, someone who in his life and work produced liminality—zones, thresholds, transitions. He avoided traditional distinctions like "masculine" and "feminine" as well as the social conventions attached to them, and he presented a world that disturbingly distanced itself from everyday understanding, from the kind of science determined by "rational" classification and obliged to "reality." His goal was to offer access to hitherto unseen, cordoned-off areas, to tap into the repressed and the taboo, and to transmit the experience of an Other, one in which there would be no distinction between reality and poetry.[12] As already suggested, Cocteau turned his creativity toward the realm of ancient mythology as part of this project. As a poet who blurred and transgressed borders, indeed as a *zonal poet* who ignored the pastness of the past, he grabbed hold of the ancient material and brought it into modernity. *La machine infernale* is a good example of this: it presents the tragic liminality of Sophocles' Oedipus comically ("de la farce") with the character of Œdipe, a hero who is no longer heroic, one who fluctuates between clumsiness and purposive rationalism. In its second act, the play dramatizes "The Encounter of Oedipus and the Sphinx" in which the protagonist—just like the Greek Oedipus in his own Sphinx encounter, but here exaggerated for intensified effect—enters a zone that is characterized spatially and figurally by indeterminacy.

By displaying the liminality of this zone in Cocteau's drama, Oedipus and the Sphinx appear together as the very image and figure of the "betwixt and between." Contained herein is an indication of the fundamental fact of human existence as that which is stretched across the span of here and there, the past and the present, the present and the future—broadly conceived, an indication of being stretched between birth and death within the horizon of an uncertainty that constitutes a basic part of human life. The constellation of Oedipus and the Sphinx is in a certain way paradigmatic for the *conditio humana*, the condition of being human and the condition of human nature, which, when driven to the limit, threatens to revert to monstrosity. And it is paradigmatic for mankind itself, which constantly strives to attain new states, forever believing that it has arrived, while being compelled to acknowledge that it remains in an ambiguous state of the "no longer" and the "not yet"—in other words, that it must tarry upon the threshold, perpetually a liminal creature.

PART ONE

Oedipus before the Sphinx in Antiquity: On Sophocles

✿

The Prince of Thebes
and the Monster

The encounter between the Sphinx and Oedipus, son of King Laius and Queen Jocasta, is part of the so-called Theban Epic Cycle, which narrates the mythical history of the Boeotian city.[1] Among the texts once belonging to this group are the *Thebaid*, of which we have a few fragments, and the *Oedipodea*, lost but for a fragment with some later testimonies regarding its contents. Both epics encompassed numerous stories arrayed around the figure of Oedipus variously represented. However, the fragmentary nature of these texts leaves it impossible to say which episodes were specifically selected for narrative unfolding or epic amplification. Instead, we have been able to reconstruct only a bare listing of what stories were included, without any sense of broader narrative development. That is to say, we learn the "what" without learning the "how." For example, we can safely assume that the *Oedipodea* contained, among other things, the episode of Oedipus' act of solving the Sphinx's riddle; but *how* precisely this story was shaped into an extended narrative is no longer extant.[2]

In addition to early references to the Oedipus myth in Hesiod's *Works and Days*, the *Iliad*, and, above all, in the Nekyia episode of the *Odyssey*, the first longer reworkings of the story date from the fifth century BCE in Attic tragedy, which drew from the early epics. Aeschylus, Sophocles, and Euripides culled various stories from the old Theban narrative tradition and adapted them for the tragic stage in accordance with the current social and political affairs in Athens. In this way, Oedipus, who until that point had been understood as a ruler defending his polis against enemy forces—thus Oedipus appears in Homer and Hesiod[3]—became *the* tragic hero par excellence.[4] Aeschylus composed a Theban tetralogy (467 BCE) that must have been of extraordinary power, since we know that it brought him victory in the *agon*. Of the four plays, only *The Seven against Thebes* has survived. Unfortunately, *Laius*, *Oedipus*, and the satyr-play *Sphinx* have been lost. The Oedipus dramatizations by Euripides and many others, including Achaeus, Philocles, and Xenocles, all written between the fifth and third centuries BCE,[5] are likewise no longer extant. Sophocles, who drew from Aeschylus among others[6] and is likely to have seen the tetralogy at around the age of thirty, has handed down to us, in addition to *Oedipus the King*, the tragedies *Antigone* and *Oedipus at Colonus*, which also address the tragic fate of Oedipus, his wife Jocasta, and their children, Antigone, Ismene, Eteocles, and Polynices.

Rendered sequentially, Oedipus' life story, in the form it had assumed in the fifth century BCE, proceeds in the following way:[7] After receiving a prophecy from the Delphic oracle that a son would be born to him at whose hand he would perish, King Laius exposes his newborn, Oedipus. Found by shepherds, the boy is taken in and raised by King Polybus and Merope in Corinth. As he grows up and begins to have doubts about his parentage, he sets out for Delphi and there receives a message from the oracle that he is fated to kill his father and marry his mother. Believing his parents to be Polybus and Merope, he resolves never to return to Corinth, journeying instead into the unknown, so as to avoid this fate. Along the way there is a violent conflict at the junction of three roads in Phocis, where Oedipus kills Laius, who unbeknownst to him is his true father. Oedipus then appears before the Sphinx, who is bringing calamity and ruin upon Thebes. He overcomes her by solving her riddle and either kills her or causes her to kill herself.[8] As a reward for this victory, Oedipus is promised sovereignty over Thebes and the hand of the widowed Queen Jocasta. He eventually realizes that she is his mother, but only after he has fathered four children with her and after a plague has come over the city. According to Apollo's proclamation, the plague will recede only when Laius' murderer is found and the crime is atoned. Through interrogating the blind seer Teiresias and learning new revelations from other sources, Oedipus at last discovers his true ancestry. Jocasta hangs herself and Oedipus stabs out his eyes. He surrenders his sovereignty and leaves Thebes to begin a wanderer's life as depicted in Sophocles' *Oedipus at Colonus*. His rapturous death at Attic Colonus alone liberates him from his homelessness. From that point on, a cult is established to venerate Oedipus as a local hero.[9]

There exists no original wording of the enigma that the Sphinx is said to have learned as a song from the Muses (Soph. *OT* 36, 130, and 391; Eur. *Phoen.* 50, 808, and 1028). A fragment by Pindar is the first text that mentions the riddle (Pind. fr. 177d Maehler). In subsequent sources, it is ordinarily transmitted in prose, although one version in hexameter is extant as well. The most reliable reconstruction of the riddle is based on a compilation of relatively late antique texts in Greek. An English translation reads: "There is a creature on earth which has two and four feet, a voice, and three feet; of all the creatures that live on earth, in the air and in the sea, it alone can change its nature. But the strength of its limbs is at its lowest precisely when it supports itself on the greatest number of feet."[10] The hexametric version, which, according to a scholion on Euripides harks back to the tragedian Asclepius (Schol. Eur. *Phoen.* 50), could have involved a quotation from the *Oedipodea* or Aeschylus' satyr-play *Sphinx*.[11] According to Pseudo-Apollodorus, the wording of the riddle was: "τί ἐστιν ὃ μίαν ἔχον φωνὴν τετράπουν καὶ δίπουν καὶ τρίπουν γίνεται; — "What is it that has a voice, and is four-, two-, and three-footed?" (Apollod. 3.5.8 [= 3.53]). The text goes on to give the solution: "Οἰδίπους δὲ ἀκούσας ἔλυσεν, εἰπὼν τὸ αἴνιγμα τὸ ὑπὸ τῆς Σφιγγὸς λεγόμενον ἄνθρωπον εἶναι· γίνεσθαι, γὰρ τετράπουν βρέφος ὄντα τοῖς τέτταρσιν ὀχούμενον κώλοις, τελειούμενον δὲ δίπουν, γηρῶντα δὲ τρίτην προσλαμβάνειν βάσιν τὸ βάκτρον—"Upon hearing this, Oedipus solved the riddle, indicating that the Sphinx intended 'man' [*anthrōpos*], who is born four-footed, crawling on all fours as an infant, but two-footed when grown up and then, with age, takes on a third foot in the form of a cane" (Apollod. 3.5.8 [= 3.54]).

A central theme in *Oedipus the King* is the human capacity for insight. It is discernible by the fact that all the essential narrative turns are known in advance. Hence, the entire sequence of events plays out not as a series of actions, but in the form of questions and answers, exploration and discovery. Two storylines—the search for Laius' murderer and the search for Oedipus' own parentage—ultimately come together in Oedipus' single, terrible recognition of his parricide and incest; and the protagonist's slow process of feeling his way toward truth, disclosure, and self-induced blindness is thereby performed.[12] Everything to be considered here, including the Sphinx episode, is related to this central theme of the human capacity for insight.

Sophocles' decision to steer attention to Oedipus' discovery of the truth—a discovery that the hero makes only through persistent, independent searching—is a reflection of the Athenian spirit of the time. In the fifth century BCE, the city-state of Athens emerged in the midst of an exceedingly active intellectual life that was coursing through the Greek-speaking realm. Sophocles was every bit as aware of its advantages as he was of its disadvantages and dangers—dangers that could reach into the abyss of human existence. As a native Athenian and great lover of his city (he bore the surname Philathenaios), Sophocles was fully integrated into the life of his time. He considered the city-state to be his task, to be fulfilled as a good citizen by taking on political as well as military offices. As Joachim Latacz expresses it, Sophocles wrote not as an entertainer but rather as "a deliberator, an advisor," as one who admonishes.[13]

We must endeavor to understand *Oedipus the King* against this background. The play appeared in 430, at the height of the Greek enlightenment movement promulgated by Sophism and its governing motto "knowledge is power" (as Francis Bacon would later formulate it). At this time, a general "euphoria of understanding" predominated, which posited, as Protagoras proclaimed, that man is "the measure of all things." Sophocles—himself a man of intelligence who, as an expression of his commitment to Athenian democracy, contributed intellectually, artistically, and politically to the social and intellectual progress of the city-state—assumed a critical position toward this worldview, insofar as he regarded it to be *one-sided*. For him, unyieldingly one-sided attitudes toward life were fundamentally disharmonic, and he saw in them the gravest danger of hubris.

Already in the prologue to *Oedipus the King*, set before the royal palace, we see clearly that the hero in his sovereign position is exposed to this danger to an especially high degree. Here, a priest who leads an emergency Theban delegation portrays for Oedipus the great need that has come upon the city as a result of the plague and beseeches him, "the first among men" (ἀνδρῶν δὲ πρῶτον, 33), for help, he who has already saved the city once before by freeing it from Sphinx's terror.[14] Oedipus appears in this scene as one endowed with thoroughly superior ability and understanding. He demonstrates that he comprehends the correct use of sense and understanding and—as Arbogast Schmitt has pointed out—that he already knows everything the priest is saying even before hearing it.[15] The opening scene's reference to Oedipus' great rescue mission as well as his intellectual prowess, which has already proven to be so beneficial to the polis, are alluded to and taken up implicitly and explicitly throughout the rest of the play, for example by the Theban seer Teiresias (*OT* 440) and by the choir of Theban elders who praise their king as having passed the Sphinx's test "cleverly" (σοφός) as a "friend of the city" (ἡδύπολις, 504–511). Here, it quickly becomes clear that Oedipus has benefited from the deed for which he became famous and from the intelligence that he applied to it. When Creon, Jocasta's brother and Oedipus' confidante, reports Apollo's pronouncement that a plague has come over the city because Laius' murderer has not been punished and the crime has not been expiated, Oedipus declares that he will "reveal" (φαίνειν) what is hidden; that is, he will bring light into the darkness of things, clear up the issue, illuminate (φανῶ) it, as he did once before by solving the Sphinx's riddle. Thus, without any hesitation, he sets himself upon this "enlightening" endeavor (*OT* 132).

This attitude—his belief in his ability to dispel the darkness of ignorance and his quick decision to act in the interest of the polis—characterizes Oedipus as a typical Athenian of the fifth century BCE, as he has been frequently depicted by modern commentators, for example, by Bernard Knox, Egon Flaig, and Hellmut Flashar. As such, he is not, therefore, unequivocally reprehensible.[16] More problematic in the

Sophoclean sense are the imbalance, disharmony, and one-sidedness apparent in Oedipus' thought and action: the hero sees his intelligence too one-sidedly as a panacea that is insuperable. He overlooks the limitations of human ability through excessive self-confidence, an oversight that, in this case, will prove deadly for the social environment that admires and enables him. He lets himself be led by strong emotions, which stand in the way of true insight and carry him away into misconduct, which he might have otherwise avoided.[17]

This fatal overconfidence reveals itself in numerous ways, but most notably in Oedipus' altercation with the blind Teiresias. Here, the king receives important information from the seer that he does not understand, not only because Teiresias, challenged by Oedipus, speaks in an emphatically prophetic language, with which he charges the riddle solver with more riddles,[18] but also because Oedipus falls into a frenzied rage strikingly fast.[19] Oedipus behaves in this scene exactly like a classic tyrant who, seeing his authority threatened by the slightest resistance, lashes out with a counterattack. When the seer, whom Oedipus had summoned for the sake of enlightenment, falls silent (since he knows the role that the king plays in Thebes' dire straits, but does not want to divulge this), the refusal to speak is regarded by Oedipus as a trace of ingratitude and insolence against the polis and against himself. He therefore promptly blames the silent seer for the murder of Laius. Teiresias will not stand for this. He counters with a volley of formidable responses, among them calling Oedipus the "land's iniquitous besmircher" (γῆς τῆσδ' ἀνοσίῳ μιάστορι, 353), declaring that he has had most heinous intercourse with his own kin (σὺν τοῖς φιλτάτοις αἴσχισθ' ὁμιλοῦντ', 366–367). Beside himself with rage, Oedipus alleges that Teiresias has conspired with Creon to plan a statewide strike to plot his fall and banishment. Oedipus announces that he will spare Teiresias from death, but he will have him exiled. As if this were not enough, he ridicules the blind man, saying that he is "lost in the dark," and demeans his "dim" soothsaying, in comparison with his own "bright" understanding (referring once again to his victory over the Sphinx). It never occurs to Oedipus that the seer, who is in contact with Apollo and receives knowledge directly from the god, refused to speak not out of ignorance but rather out of wisdom. Oedipus questions Teiresias on his capabilities: Where has he proven himself a seer? Why did he not pronounce the saving word when the Sphinx—that "female singer" (ἡ ῥαψῳδός), that "bitch" (κύων, 391)—was here? At that time, the gift of prophecy, which clearly he did not possess, having learned it neither from birds nor from a god, was desperately needed; and he, Oedipus, had to come in order to dispatch the Sphinx, to "stop her" (ἔπαυσά νιν, 397), to strike her down "with intelligence not taught by birds" (γνώμῃ κυρήσας οὐδ' ἀπ' οἰωνῶν μαθών, 398). Without a doubt, Oedipus gives himself over to pride in his own autonomous knowledge, convinced that he has no need for any higher inspiration. Jochen Schmidt has taken this scene as occasion to read an anti-enlightenment character into the drama. With the riddle solver Oedipus, who first climbs high and then plummets down, Sophocles has brought a representative figure of the Athenian enlightenment before our eyes. It must have been the tragedian's intention "to save the reputation of certain religious institutions, namely soothsaying and the nature of the oracle, from the doubt that stems from the advances of enlightenment."[20]

Face-to-Face: Oedipus before the Sphinx in the Vase Painting of Antiquity

In the confrontation between Oedipus and Teiresias, as in other places where the Sphinx is mentioned in *Oedipus the King*, we receive no precise information about the Sphinx herself, nor about the nature of Oedipus' encounter with her. We can only presume that she was a "singer"—ῥαψῳδός—who chanted her riddle, possibly like an oracle.[21] In his boastful account, Oedipus drops most of the details of the encounter and merely reminds Teiresias that it was he who brought the bitch (κύων) to silence with his own power (*OT* 397–398)—that is, with his γνώμη—a term that has been variously interpreted as "wit" (Knox; Schadewaldt [*Witz*]), "head" (Weinstock [*Kopf*]), "sense" (Wilamowitz [*Sinn*]), "understanding" (Willige [*Verstand*]), or "intelligence" (Grene).[22] Apart from this, we learn nothing else. Concerning the precise way in which the encounter unfolded—the details of the setting, the Sphinx's physical appearance—there is a decided gap in the drama.[23]

Nevertheless, it would be a mistake to conclude from this sparse account that the encounter with the Sphinx, well known from old saga cycles, was not widely disseminated or that it was unpopular in Athens at the time. For one, Sophocles does not merely mention the episode in passing, but rather alludes to it again and again throughout his tragedy. Beyond this, we have illuminating archeological evidence that resolves any lingering question of the episode's import. Indeed, in *Oedipus the King*, the proof of the hero's intelligence is directly and repeatedly tied to this encounter, and his victory over the Sphinx is precisely what earns him the admiration of his people.[24] This attests to the encounter's significance within the tragedy, but it does not account for its significance within the broader cultural context.

Sophocles could well have deployed the figure of the Sphinx simply for the sake of establishing and emphasizing Oedipus' identity as a highly astute man, even if the encounter had not had a firm place in Greek narrative lore of the fifth century BCE. But the archaeological findings that I will discuss here prove that the *rencontre* did indeed have such a place: Oedipus before the Sphinx is not only one of many figured constellations frequently depicted from Greek mythology; among the multiple motifs surrounding the Oedipus figure, it is by far the most commonly depicted of all. Of the roughly one hundred images of the hero that are known to us (predominately painted on vases), over 70 percent feature this scene, and roughly 40 percent come from the fifth century BCE, from the time before *Oedipus the King*.[25] Thus we can be certain that this scene, especially in Athens, was well known when Sophocles was writing his play, that it was indeed the privileged visual motif among those representing Oedipus' life story. Aeschylus' Theban tetralogy from 476 BCE, with its undoubtedly spectacular satyr-play *Sphinx*, may have contributed to this popularity.[26] In any case, in Athens, where depictions of Oedipus had begun to appear around 540/530, the figured constellation of Oedipus before the Sphinx became iconographically prevalent between 470 and 450. As vase painting, plastic and mosaic art, sarcophagi, and gems all document, it soon became the most commonly depicted scene of the Oedipus myth, and remained so for the rest of antiquity. At first, in early representations, Oedipus had been regularly accompanied by other figures, mainly Thebans (often in the midst of Theban assemblies, possibly as part of a new trend that favored images of debating citizens within the newly instituted Attic democracy); yet, by the second quarter of the fifth century, he was almost always alone, dressed as a wanderer or a traveler (with a staff, or two spears, a hat, and a cloak), positioned across from the Sphinx, with both figures in profile.

The two oldest, entirely intact vessels featuring Oedipus alone before the Sphinx are, first, an Attic red-figured krater from around 480/470 BCE,[27] which shows Oedipus standing and supported by a long walking stick, looking at the Sphinx straight in the face; and second, a red-figured *kylix* dating from the same time,[28] which displays an image fraught with tension, where the Sphinx, ready to pounce on her seated opponent, voices her riddle (the two words [K]ΑΙ ΤΡΙ[ΠΟΥΝ], "and three-footed," may be seen before her mouth, which nonetheless is closed), while the hero in travel attire sits pondering, an image of intense concentration, face-to-face with the Sphinx (fig. 1).[29]

Numerous images from the following decades (and centuries) follow this basic visual pattern. Although occasionally sitting, Oedipus mostly stands pondering before the Sphinx, who sits across from him atop columns or pillars, sometimes on altar-like shapes of varying heights or up on rocks. He always looks her in the eyes, whether he finds himself at her eye level, whether he is higher than her or she higher than him. This frontal gaze is significant and deserves special attention; for it is through this frontality that Oedipus determines his position with regard to the inhuman and the superhuman. Thus, using his gifts of understanding, he alights upon the riddle's solution, "man." From this point forward, the idea of Oedipus' frontal position across from the Sphinx will continually reenter the discussion in new and developing ways.

Alongside the riddle scene, we find some combat scenes in which Oedipus points his spear at the Sphinx. Still, in terms of sheer quantity, frontally arranged images that do not suggest physical or armed violence clearly predominate. As in Sophocles, the hero generally confronts the Sphinx solely "with the power of his mind" (γνώμη). As indicated above, the Athens of the fifth century was preoccupied with this very idea: that is, with the development of an intelligence independent of old, mythic conceptions of might and impotence. By the power of thought, man hoped to confront uncanny, inhuman, threatening forces, to "face up to them" in a quasi-literal sense, and to over-

FIG. 1. Oedipus seated on a rock ponders the riddle of the Theban Sphinx. Attic red-figure *kylix*, c. 480/470 BC, Museo Gregoriano Etrusco, attributed to the so-called Oedipus Painter.

come them through understanding rather than brute force.[30] Accordingly, images of Oedipus only occasionally depict a physically superior warrior. Much more commonly they show not a zealous hero fighting bravely to defend Thebes, but rather an astute man who confronts an uncanny creature and refuses to avert his gaze until his powers of understanding have guaranteed him victory.

When spectators at the original performances of *Oedipus the King* heard the words that Oedipus chose to describe his encounter with the Sphinx (ἔπαυσά νιν / γνώμῃ κυρήσας), they must have immediately thought of the iconically familiar, standard version of this confrontation between the poser and solver of the riddle. In the narrative context conjured by the play's verses and reinforced by its constellation of images, they must have been reminded of Oedipus' great and unambiguous victory over the monster. But all those who had understood the story as being exclusively about the radiant victory of intelligence—which was the predominantly popular reading at the time—were about to have their expectations formidably checked by Sophocles' version. His tragedy presented before the eyes of an Athenian audience how the intelligence of the hero—such a positive trait in and of itself—could swell into something negative. Thus, the tragic representation significantly tarnished the hero's gleaming reputation that by Sophocles' day was already legendary, as evident in the proverbial "wisdom of Oedipus" celebrated by Pindar (*Pyth.* 4.263). Confident in the might of his intelligence—a belief acknowledged by all those around him—Sophocles' Oedipus rashly condemns Teiresias' pronouncement without even considering it.[31] In brief, what the Chorus offers for reflection becomes frighteningly apparent, that "those hasty to decide falter all too easily" (φρονεῖν γὰρ οἱ ταχεῖς οὐκ ἀσφαλεῖς, *OT* 617).

That the powers of "one led astray by his own cleverness"[32] are superior to the conventional powers of the seer—a conviction that Oedipus believes was confirmed by his victory over the Sphinx—proves itself at the play's end to have been an incorrect self-assessment, a delusion (ἄτη), and ultimately an act of self-overestimation (ὕβρις). The Oedipus that Sophocles stages is a man who relies *one-sidedly* on his intelligence. This overreliance is, in the sense of Aristotelian theory of tragedy, his ἁμαρτία (his "tragic flaw" or, better, his "misaim"—

"that which he lacks [in the pursuit of something]," *Poet.* 1453a10f.). Indeed, Oedipus relies on an intelligence that leads him into catastrophe (καταστροφή, "turning toward demise"), in which his identity as a man whose intelligence makes him unconquerable breaks down. This is not the place to take up the debate over guilt and innocence in this story, a debate that has reached no consensus over the last 250 years.[33] Suffice it to say that, in my view, the drama is thoroughly engaged with considerations of responsibility, and is in no way *primarily* about the powerlessness of humanity and the illusory nature of human existence—an opinion that Karl Reinhardt supported in his influential 1933 Sophocles book.[34] I likewise see no indications that Sophocles intended to represent Oedipus—as Wolfgang Schadewaldt put it—as "one of the noblest of men."[35] Rather, the hero of *Oedipus the King* exhibits markedly destructive and misguided inclinations, as exemplified by his conflict with Teiresias and his subsequent, overconfident boast that he is the one and only "true seer." As Wolfgang Kullmann plausibly formulates it, "It may always be the case that a degree of guilt accompanies those who meet their doom at the hands of the gods."[36] At any rate, what cannot be doubted—and what the play's concluding choral song makes perfectly clear—is that with this dramatic presentation of the tragic plot Sophocles once again comes forward as an admonisher:

ὦ πάτρας Θήβης ἔνοικοι, λεύσσετ', Οἰδίπους ὅδε,
ὃς τὰ κλείν' αἰνίγματ' ᾔδει καὶ κράτιστος ἦν ἀνήρ,
οὗ τίς οὐ ζήλῳ πολιτῶν ἦν τύχαις ἐπιβλέπων,
εἰς ὅσον κλύδωνα δεινῆς συμφορᾶς ἐλήλυθεν.
ὥστε θνητὸν ὄντα κείνην τὴν τελευταίαν ἰδεῖν
ἡμέραν ἐπισκοποῦντα μηδέν' ὀλβίζειν, πρὶν ἂν
τέρμα τοῦ βίου περάσῃ μηδὲν ἀλγεινὸν παθών.

Residents of our native Thebes, behold, this is Oedipus, who knew the renowned riddle, and was a most mighty man. What citizen did not gaze on his fortune with envy? See into what a stormy sea of troubles he has come! Therefore, while our eyes wait to see the final destined day, we must call no mortal happy until he has crossed life's border free from pain.[37]

About five hundred years after Oedipus' tragedy was performed in Athens, Seneca the Younger, master of the ghastly and the grotesque, filled the gap in Sophocles' drama by detailing the outcome of the Sphinx encounter. The tragedy that Seneca created is the second major treatment of this material that has reached us from antiquity. Seneca's *Oedipus* breaks up the systematic narrative structure of *Oedipus the King* into a series of blocks of action with tableaus inserted between. The Sphinx episode is portrayed in some detail. Like Sophocles, Seneca uses the artistic device of retrospective to bring this scene into the play. Yet, distinguishing himself from the Greek playwright, he gives substantially more information about the event's location and the Sphinx's appearance. The hero's mythic encounter with the *monstrum* (*Oed.* 106) serves, as numerous scenes of his affect-laden horror dramas often do, to intensify the atmosphere of darkness and demise, which furnishes the backdrop of the entire play.[38] Here and throughout, the impression is conveyed that the world of the living and the world of the dead, earth and hell, can no longer be held separate. In a conversation with Jocasta at the play's opening, Oedipus' retrospective account of his encounter with the Sphinx begins with a vivid description of the *monstrum*'s lair. He tells how the Sphinx ambushes her prey from up on high cliffs (*e superna rupe*), under which the ground shimmers white (*albens*) with strewn bones (*ossibus sparsis*). Just as in the Siren episode in Homer's *Odyssey*, which, with equally bleak imagery, insinuates the lack of funeral rites for murdered men,[39] Seneca here evokes a topography of dread, which the following description intensifies: In the encounter with Oedipus, the Sphinx held her wings (*alas*) at the ready, threw the whip of her tail (*caudae*) into motion, like that of a fierce lion (*saevi leonis more*), and, with threats (*minas*) pouring forth through her clenched jaw, she let her sad song (*triste carmen*) nightmarishly (*horrendum*) ring out. Impatiently slavering for Oedipus' entrails, she scraped at the rocks with her claws (*unguis*), knocking off debris.[40] Seneca's version of the encounter became canonical, and in the sense of a "littérature au second degré," unfolded a high level of secondary productivity through its intertextual relation with subsequent modern texts.[41]

After centuries of influencing European literature and art, the Sphinx episode inspired Cocteau to dedicate the entire second act of *La machine infernale* to it. His elaborate treatment of the mythic constellation, as well as the manifold ways in which it informed the rest of his literary, filmic, and imagistic production, makes clear that Cocteau, like Seneca, saw Sophocles' sparse treatment of the episode as a welcome gap, as an invitation to expand. Well versed in modern mythography, Cocteau knew exactly how to fill this space, and in a way far more exhaustive than Seneca's attempts.

Admittedly, we must remember that *La machine infernale* as well as Cocteau's other reworkings of *Oedipus the King* were preceded by a great body of "literature from literature," for example, the *Oedipus* tragedies of Corneille (1659) and Voltaire (1718), all of which bring Sophocles' and Seneca's works into the modern and contemporary eras.[42] Many such works, including Corneille's version of the encounter, are based primarily on Sophocles, but they clearly draw from Seneca as well. The encounter with the "Monstre" is presented here, as in the old Greek and Latin versions of the tragedy, through the hero's retrospective account (*Œdipe* 246–253), in which—and this is the moment that reminds us of Seneca—the event takes place at the foot of a "horrid" cliff, strewn with bleaching bones: "Au pied du roc affreux semé d'os blanchissants, / Je demande l'Énigme."[43] Seneca's eerie take on the scene may well have had an effect on Corneille's famous *Œdipe* as well as on Cocteau, even if not directly. Cocteau wrote a Sphinx-Nemesis character into *La machine infernale*, which, as we will see, could behave in an utterly terrifying way. At any rate, these reworkings of the Oedipus material, up through Cocteau, show the particularly influential effect of *Oedipus the King*, all the way into the modern era.[44] Cocteau's achievement is to have singled out the Sphinx episode from among all of the Theban narratives surrounding Oedipus, and to have used it to fill the dramatic gap that Sophocles left empty.

CHAPTER TWO

Thresholds:
Zone, Transformation, Transition

Apart from a few scattered reflections, the key function of the Sphinx episode has been neglected in the scholarship. That is not to say that the importance of Oedipus' encounter has not been recognized. In his article "Sphinx" for the 1929 edition of the Pauly-Wissowa encyclopedia, Albin Lesky made it clear that this episode plays a significant role in the onward progression of the story, since Oedipus is able to assume sovereignty over Thebes only after winning this victory over the Sphinx. Extrapolating from the fact that the "Sphinx saga" is much older than the "epic narrative, which integrated it into the frame of the Oedipus myth," Lesky sees the "task of the Sphinx story" within the epic framework to "afford Oedipus the opportunity to win the prize, Jocasta's hand, by overcoming the monster."[1] Like L. W. Daly in his Pauly-Wissowa article on "Oedipus," Lesky leads the Oedipus story back to old fairy tale lore.[2]

Such considerations concerning the origins of the Oedipus story and the Sphinx episode are in no way unique to ancient studies and were already entertained in different disciplinary contexts well before Lesky. For example in 1922 Martin P. Nilsson challenged Carl Roberts' thesis that the Oedipus figure represents a seasonal god[3] and instead adopts the view that the story is in principle a fairy tale about a hero who wins the hand of a princess by accomplishing a valiant deed.[4] This theme was also taken up in the second half of the twentieth century, notably and comprehensively by Ulrich Hausmann and Lowell Edmunds. Both grappled with the question of the relation between the Sphinx and the larger Oedipus plot, that is, whether the riddle episode constituted an original part of the Oedipus story, displaying a fairy tale structure. Both arrived at utterly divergent responses. Upon comparing numerous archaeological and literary testaments, Hausmann concluded that the "Sphinx-motif" was "inseparably bound up with the Oedipus saga," and that "the conquest over the Sphinx" should be regarded as a "hinge between murdering the father and marrying the mother" and belonged "since time immemorial at the apex of Oedipus' illustrious rise." As he saw it, the narrative of this ascent employs a conventional "fairy tale topos": a hero comes upon a land devastated by a vicious beast and ruled by a helpless widow; by freeing the land, he marries the widow and thereby attains sovereignty. According to Hausmann, through a specific link with Thebes, the tale was transferred into the sphere of hero mythology and further linked to the incest motif.[5] In contrast, Edmunds essentially rehearsed Lesky's view. In adopting the index that Antti Aarne and Stith Thompson developed for classifying folktales and in light of Vladimir Propp's essay "Oedipus in the Light of Folklore,"[6] Edmunds comes to the conclusion that there is a difference to be drawn between the "Dragon-Slayer" (Type 300: the hero slays a monster and wins the hand of the princess), and Oedipus (Type 931). He thus argued that the Sphinx motif does not belong to the intrinsic core of the Oedipus tale, namely the parricide and the mother-incest. Rather, the Sphinx motif constitutes a secondary element, "added at some point in the development of the legend in order to motivate the hero's marriage to his mother."[7]

The issues broached by Hausmann and Edmunds concerning the episode's origin will not be pursued further here. Rather, we will take up what the vase paintings make especially clear and what most studies on the Oedipus-Sphinx thematic allow us to recognize: namely, that the

Sphinx episode was an altogether important part of the Oedipus story by the fifth century BCE at the latest and has remained so across the centuries. The "task of the Sphinx story" within the prevailing narrative is in no way exhausted in its function as a structural element that guarantees the plot's progress, as Claude Lévi-Strauss, for example, famously suggested in his well-known analysis of Oedipus in "The Structural Study of Myth" (1955).[8] Rather, the episode should be appreciated as far more significant than it has been until now. We can go past Lesky's reflections on the "task of the Sphinx story" within the "saga's fabric" if we turn our attention to the topographic space designed by the narrative. The topography is composed of overlapping frames: first, the Sphinx story, which encompasses the figure of the Sphinx and her location; and second, the larger scheme of the Oedipus story, which includes the Sphinx material. Involved here is a specific mytho-topography that organizes myth in space and space in myth. What is designed is first a space before the city of Thebes: comprehensible as a real, tangible geography, but expanded into the realm of the speculative and the imaginary through the Sphinx's haunting presence. Second, there is the space of the *zone*, the *threshold*, and the *transition*, both in terms of how it is described and in terms of the mythic events that happen there. As the following remarks will clarify, the Sphinx episode serves as the transition between the events that take place narratively and topographically outside Thebes (Oedipus' exposure as an infant up through the first broken taboo, the murder of his father) and the events that take place inside Thebes (his marriage to his mother, the second broken taboo, up through his final renunciation of Thebes as a grown man, the moment of what could be called his "re-exposure.") The Sphinx episode is thus a linking joint in the narrative that mythographically generates an intervening space, a threshold, a zone. It is also a pivot point, upon which the major remaining narrative segments are symmetrically arranged, indeed, upon which they revolve, using this episode as their fulcrum: it brings the first major segment of narrated events outside Thebes (taboo 1: "exposure" and "parricide") into a mirror-image relationship with the second major segment (taboo 2: "mother incest" and Oedipus' "re-exposure"), without making the two parts identical.

Outside Thebes	*Exposure* as newborn
	Further events (several years)
	Parricide (taboo 1)

Threshold, Zone	*Confrontation with the Sphinx*

	Mother-incest (taboo 2)
Inside Thebes	Further events (several years)
	Re-exposure as grown man

The fulcrum function also exhibits a referential function, which allows the zonal episode to work as a metanarrative of the larger story in which it is embedded. As a threshold characterized by a threshold figure, the "Sphinx-story" narratively marks "what the story is about" in the version of the Oedipus myth as it is handed down and canonized, so to speak, by Sophocles: it presents — according to Greek notions — a scandalously liminal being, perceived as a socially intolerable existence at the threshold. What the Sphinx's monstrous presence makes clear, then, is that she is a metafigure for Oedipus' entire condition. He is perhaps not as conspicuous as she, but his existence similarly infects the Greek world order with a deviant, disturbing, marginal element. Exposed as a child, he bears a mark. The name Οἰδίπους may be variously interpreted;[9] in terms of the myth, it is the piercing of his infant feet at the time of his exposure that earned him the name "Swollen-Foot."[10] Thus, with scarred feet, he is marked off as a double breaker of taboos.

Due to the fundamental dynamics of life, dynamics that necessitate spatial, temporal, and social transitions, stories of this nature are to be found in all the world's cultures, not only in Greek antiquity or in later European contexts. Oedipus' story is the story of a man who seems to have mastered an existentially significant step over a threshold, a transition to be completed. *Externally*, he performs this task with certain bravery and success; yet *internally*, the mission is incomplete. Although he moves past the Sphinx, victorious and therefore seemingly postliminal, he is in fact perpetually liminal, for internally he remains trapped within a threshold existence, outside the borders of the society in which he lives. In the end, as he recognizes this inescapable, *internal* liminality, he draws, according to Sophocles, the consequences and renders himself *externally* visible as a threshold being by blinding himself and then, as an abomination to himself and to others, by leaving the city along with all human community behind.

In German it is especially clear that the "threshold" (*Schwelle*) is the *swollen* part of the doorway. The present remarks consider the referential function of the Sphinx episode as a threshold story (*Schwellengeschichte*) within the story of "Threshold or Swollen Foot" (*Schwellfuß*): they address the task of the episode as a narrative marker (and the function of the Sphinx as a figurative marker) of Oedipus' liminality. These reflections are oriented, among others, by the prominent determination of the threshold that Walter Benjamin postulates in the *Arcades Project*: "The threshold [*Schwelle*] must be very sharply distinguished from the border [*Grenze*]. The threshold is a zone. Transformation, transition, floods lie in the word 'swelling' [*schwellen*] and etymology ought not to overlook these senses."[11] Extrapolating from Benjamin, I see the distinction between *border* and *threshold* as lying, above all, in the distinction between fixed and porous boundaries. Whereas every border seeks to distinguish or discriminate, and hence establish absolute definitions and binary structures, the threshold, through its "in between" positioning, marks out an area shared by both sides. Situated in between, the threshold constitutes a zone of equivocity and ambiguity, a place where boundaries are dissolved, where one side passes into the other. This special quality of the threshold confirms the research of ritual by the ethnologists Arnold van Gennep and Victor Turner, whose studies on "Threshold Beings" and "Threshold States" pertain to what Turner characterized as the concept of "liminality."

"Betwixt and Between": The Threshold Theories of Arnold van Gennep and Victor Turner

Arnold van Gennep's studies form the basis of the liminality scholarship that Victor Turner furthered decades later. Van Gennep's book, *Les rites de passage* (1909), considers rituals from numerous geographic regions and historical periods, dealing in each case with the transition from one socially defined area of life to another.[12] Adducing van Gennep's theory for a reading of the Oedipus myth immediately offers itself, since the case of the Theban hero involves a transition in manifold ways, including the territorial—the transition from youth to manhood, from bachelorhood to marriage, from outsider to citizen— hence, it involves precisely the kinds of transitions that van Gennep explored. Since the idea of transition is evident across the Oedipus myth, researchers have repeatedly connected it with initiation. The work of Louis Gernet, founder of the historical anthropological study of antiquity, broached this trend by speaking of an "initiation royale," followed by the work of Marie Delcourt and Vladimir Propp, among others.[13] For example, Ulrich Hausmann, discussed above, considers the Oedipus story with reference to puberty rituals of diverse cultures. Similarly, Jan Bremmer reads the myth as a narrative expansion of the incest motif belonging to the narrative type "young man becomes a king or culture hero."[14] This type appears to be accentuated by Sophocles, which points to a problematic societal structure in fifth-century Athens. In most of the studies that likewise see an element of initiation in the Oedipus myth, the Sphinx episode is taken to be a life-and-death trial, one that the hero must pass in order to arrive back in Thebes and become king or culture hero. And yet the episode's precise significance as a threshold moment within the narrative of the hero's scandalously liminal existence has remained unrecognized. This significance comes noticeably to the fore in reading van Gennep and Turner, above all their discussion of the "threshold phase," which both regard as a central component in every *rite de passage*, and which is of particular relevance for the present considerations.

Van Gennep's point of departure is the observation that societies are fundamentally composed of numerous and disparate social groups separated by various factors (family, locality, age, profession, religion, political allegiances, etc.), and that, in reference to the dynamics of life, every society must contend with changes in these group affiliations and delineations. The purpose of regulations is to avert the danger of possible disturbances to the statically conceived social order, to avert the peril that results from the dynamics of these changes, which lie in the intermediate state, where an individual belongs neither to one group nor to any other. It is precisely this intermediate state that most interests us here. Van Gennep posits a three-phase structural model: a detachment phase, in which group affiliation is to change; a threshold phase, an undefined moment that is especially vulnerable to influence from any and all possible sources; and finally, an integration phase, in which the individual at last assumes a new identity. Three rites correspond to transitions in the life of an individual, from one stage to the next, to a new social position, and so forth: preliminary rites of separation from a previous world (*rites de séparation*); rites of the threshold or conversion (*rites de marge*); and rites of becoming a renewed member of a community (*rites d'agrégation*). Each rite symbolizes transitions in various ways, for example, through seclusion in a hut, through symbolic positioning on a threshold or in a particular zone, through stepping over a borderline, and so forth. Within a transition rite, components can receive differing emphases, depending on the case at hand. In his study, van Gennep chooses spatial transitions as a model for all transitions, first because they are a common element of many transition rites (such as birth, initiation, marriage, funerary, and seasonal ritual events), and, second, because transition rites are fundamentally based on some kind of literal going over, experienced as a change in one's state of being, as a kind of death and rebirth. He argues that the symbolic acts of these ritual events contain, accordingly, many spatial aspects. Through "dispossession," the *rites de séparation* may require removal of clothing, or relocation to a place outside the town in order to signal the dissolution of a previously clear, fixed condition. The *rites d'agrégation*, through analogous acts like reentry into the town, the putting on of new clothing, the exchange of gifts, or ritual sexual intercourse, express a new position in life, one that is once again clearly defined. In the *rites de marge*, which can be divided into threshold rites (relating to a change in place) and conversion rites (relating to a change in state of being), the individual is in a situation that van Gennep likens to a no-man's-land. The individual literally "wavers between two worlds," a state that the rite expresses both spatially and symbolically.[15] For example, analogous to an inner retreat in the midst of a chaotic situation, participants in the ritual event linger on land, city, neighborhood, town, temple, or house borders, that is, in a sanctified "neutral zone," a cordoned-off territory like those spaces marked off in antiquity by border stones, walls, and statues.[16] The initiates must linger at a point between where they were and where the rite is designed to take them. Only after spending time in this zone—that is, only after having stood on the threshold—can they finally cross over and in through a door, gate, or portal on the far side.[17] It is not enough simply to pass the threshold; anyone wishing to complete the transition must interact with the threshold as its own distinct, crucial aspect of the experience.

Victor Turner extensively attends these transition phases, deepening van Gennep's theoretical and systematic claims, in his essay "Betwixt and Between" (1967) and in *The Ritual Process* (1969).[18] According to Turner, the threshold phase is the most important part, since it forms the lynchpin of transformation from one phase into another. It is distinctive, for it is the condition of being "betwixt and between": between and amid two precisely defined states, in a state of indeterminacy outside of socially accepted boundaries. It is marked by general uncertainty, lack of structure, and ambiguity, as Turner shows with examples from initiation rites that place special stress and emphasis on this phase. People in this state are neither one thing nor another, which, especially with pubescent teenagers, often expresses itself in an extreme reduction or exaggeration in the individual's range of social behavior. It is precisely these kinds of changes that are ritually dramatized in ceremonies. To demonstrate that they possess no status and no property, participants in the ritual must submit to nakedness, endure the most severe physical and psychic stress, and withstand long periods of seclusion and isolation, in which they may be sequestered in a secret location, cast out into the wilderness, or disguised behind masks, costumes, or body paint. Turner explains that the "threshold state" (liminality), and these "threshold people" (border walkers), "slip through the network of classifications that normally locate states and position in cultural space": "Liminal entities are neither here nor there; they are betwixt and between the positions assigned and arrayed by law, custom, convention, and ceremony."[19] This means that all usual economic and legal relations are changed in the threshold phase, sometimes even rendered moot. Social rules belonging to the "world" from which the separation takes place as well as those belonging to the other "world" about to be introduced are no longer or not yet valid. Classifying conclusions on the position of the person or the group, either in the prior social structure or in the one that will subsequently predominate, is impossible.

Van Gennep sees the threshold of the entryway into a house or into a temple as exemplary of this state, marking and symbolizing the transition between public and private, or between profane and sacred, spaces. "Guardians of the threshold" are especially significant for him, as they tended to "take on monumental proportions, as in Egypt, in Assyrio-Babylonia," as "winged dragons, the sphinx, and all sorts of monsters."[20] He understands these guardians to be earthly incarnations of the threshold's supernatural qualities. They are living embodiments of threshold forces, and, receptive to prayers and sacrifices, they safeguard the transition. Through their numinous presence, they push the earthly, spatial aspect of the door and the threshold into the background, and they foreground the spookier, more abstract qualities of these liminal spaces.

It comes as no surprise, then, that van Gennep mentions "Egypt" and "Assyrio-Babylonia" in the same place where he conjures the Sphinx. Although the Sphinx of the Oedipus tale is also a perfect figure of ambiguity, and although the area outside Thebes in which she lives can be seen as a sacred "neutral zone," in the sense that van Gennep describes it, there are crucial differences between the Sphinx of Egypt and the Middle East, on the one hand, and the Sphinx in the cultural region of Greece on the other, especially when it comes to the so-called Theban Sphinx.[21] Ultimately, by the time of its incorporation into the Theban legends, this numinous protector of sanctuaries transformed into a being reputed to perpetrate bloody terror, thus posing a threat to the social order. The urgent task now was to bring this menace to an end. Thus, the Theban Sphinx in the Greek imagination was not a numinous guardian, as van Gennep understood the Egyptian and Middle Eastern Sphinx to be, namely as a creature to whom prayers and offerings are presented in exchange for safe passage; rather, she was understood as a figure whose appearance *in corpore* represented the very threat to be avoided—the possible dangers of the threshold that anyone moving from one side or state to another had to pass through. Instead of mediating between these dangers for the person passing over, she now *was* the danger, concentrated into a single body.

Whoever encountered the Sphinx was confronted with the monstrous embodiment of the threshold phase's negative aspects, the potential dangers that threatened everyone who made the passage. He confronted an exemplary threshold figure, an in-between being marked by indeterminacy, which he had to brave as an Other and, at the same time, as the double of himself (more on this below). While looking into this creature's face, he saw the very thing that needed to be exorcised, the negative social potential within himself, with the risk of being torn asunder from himself, of getting lost in the sphere of this creature. This was exactly Oedipus' experience, according to the Greek sources from the fifth century BCE: a foreigner from Corinth, he approached with courage and acumen what terrified the citizens of Thebes. He confronted the Sphinx head-on, coming right into the sphere of her power, without losing himself in it as those before him had. Rather, pondering the face of the Sphinx as it appeared before him, he found himself there, realizing that he himself was the "man" of the riddle's solution. Because of this incredible, singular insight, Oedipus believed that he would always be up to such a challenge, that he had within him a force superior to the danger posed by this liminal being. And thus he entered the city, where he was celebrated as the repairer of order, as a man of valiant civic spirit, someone worthy of the Theban throne.

A "Double-Formed Monster" (δίμορφον θηρίον): The Sphinx as Threshold Figure in Antiquity

Many features of the Sphinx revealed her to be a threshold being, a figure of the "betwixt and between" par excellence. The most conspicuous of these was her physical appearance, which mixed and blurred the defining categories of the Greek world. Appearing in almost all ancient cultures, the Sphinx is a primordial Gestalt type with a lion's body and a human head, one that archeology unsurprisingly terms a "human-headed lion." Neither human nor animal, but rather both at once and therefore more than both, this type tells of the privilege of the gods to be capable of being otherwise, of their superior status and their special power. Its existence reaches back to the beginnings of the ancient Egyptian kingdom; and, in the course of the development of

Egyptian culture, it came to symbolize either godliness or likeness to the Pharaoh or both.[22] The best known Egyptian Sphinx is, of course, the 20-meter-high, 73.5-meter-long colossus in front of the pyramids of the Pharaohs Cheops and Chephren in Giza. Up to this day, no one knows for certain what the hybrid's function there was. New suppositions continue to appear. Perhaps it was meant to guard the plateau of Giza. At any rate, the Sphinx eventually found her way into Greek iconography via Crete, where a specific Cretan-Minoan type evolved, based on Egyptian and Near Eastern suggestions.[23] From here, in the late eighth century BCE, around the end of the Geometric and the beginning of the Orientalizing Period, the Sphinx moved into Greek iconography.[24] Also belonging to this image repertoire from the second half of the sixth century BCE was the "Theban Sphinx," as the Gestalt-type entered Greek mythography.[25]

The changes that the Sphinx underwent during this decontextualizing shift to Greece were numerous. Among these she acquired functions as a harbinger of death and as its witness.[26] Another related development was a shift in gender: whereas the Egyptian Sphinx had been primarily male, the figure was increasingly represented as female. Later, in Greek mythology, the Sphinx assumed a decisively feminine character. In the Greek images that have reached us from the sixth century BCE, the Sphinx regularly appears with a human head or upper body, and a lion's lower body with wings. Whereas until the end of the sixth century BCE the feminine gender could only be deduced *ex negativo*—as some male features like the beard and the helmet started to disappear—in the fifth century, female accentuation through breasts became common, even if it was still not obligatory. This was definitely true of the Theban Sphinx, whom Euripides portrayed as the "flying girl" (τὸ παρθένιον πτερόν).[27] According to Pseudo-Apollodorus's *Library*, she had a woman's face (πρόσωπον γυναικός), the chest, feet, and tail of a lion (στῆθος καὶ βάσιν καὶ οὐρὰν λέοντος), and the wings of a bird (πτέρυγας ὄρνιθος).[28] Diodorus Siculus related her monstrous appearance to the thought-provoking duplicity formula δίμορφον θηρίον ("double-formed monster"). In his rendering of the Oedipus narrative, Diodorus writes that one told the myth that a Sphinx, a "double-formed monster," had come to Thebes: μυθολογοῦσι σφίγγα, δίμορφον θηρίον, παραγενομένην εἰς τὰς Θήβας.[29] By this point, it was no longer the case that her deviation from physical and recognizably human integrity was a mark of distinction and proof of a superior—godly—state of being, as it had been suggested in earlier Greek receptions of the Egyptian Sphinx type. Here, it concerns rather a scandal in the order of things, which embodies what threatens, as it were, to disintegrate mankind, precisely on the basis of its participation in the monstrous.

Genealogical accounts, as Hesiod and other Greco-Roman mythographers present them to us,[30] come into the picture and also testify to the Sphinx's "liminal character." According to Pseudo-Apollodorus and Hyginus,[31] the winged lion-woman was the daughter of the snake-woman Echidna and Typhon,[32] said to have the heads of a hundred snakes. Alternatively, her birth may have been the product of incest: her mother being Echidna's daughter Chimaera,[33] the fire-spitting creature with lion-, goat-, and snake-heads, and, according to Hesiod, her father being Orthos, the two-headed dog, son of Echidna and therefore Chimaera's brother.[34] It is also significant that Euripides (like Herodotus)[35] referred to her with the epithet Μ[ε]ιξοπάρθενος ("half virgin"), the same epithet that he used for Echidna, which attests to her status as a child of the earth and of the Echidna line, supposedly sent up from the underworld by Hades himself.[36] The fact that her true genealogy is so hard to determine, and that radically divergent family lines all claim her as their own, already characterizes her origins as liminal. She is, so to speak, a child of the threshold; this much, and no more, is clear. All of her possible family members threaten the normal form and proportions of the human body and the larger sphere of normally defined society. Every purported progenitor has a gross surplus of limbs, heads, and voices, to the point of redundancy. Representing the earth's primal violence, they are beings at once fearsomely destructive and fearsomely fertile. To be a member of the Echidna line is to be χθόνιος ("of the soil, associated with the underworld"), to possess earthy powers, which, in their chaotic nature, pose a threat to human existence.

As Jean-Pierre Vernant, among others, has construed it, these chthonic beings represent the darkest, most benighted aspects of the world. Olympian Zeus endeavored to eradicate them, to haul them altogether out of the world, or to sequester them where they belonged, in the deepest of deeps, for the sake of establishing what he intended to be a light-filled dominion over a well-ordered universe.[37] Thus, to subdue and rule over their primal violence and disorder, their volatility and confusion, required no less a feat than "bringing the world into order." Hesiod described Echidna in the *Theogony* as an "untamable," one part quick-eyed, beautiful-cheeked girl (ἥμισυ μὲν νύμφην ἑλικώπιδα καλλιπάρῃον), one part monstrous snake (ἥμισυ πέλωρον ὄφιν), violent, big, and ravenous, writhing wildly in the depths of the holy earth: δεινόν τε μέγαν τε αἰόλον ὠμηστὴν ζαθέης ὑπὸ κεύθεσι γαίης.[38] In Hesiod's account, she resides on the outer edge of the known world, with the Arimoi in Lydia. According to Herodotus, she resides with the Scythians, since the Greeks regarded her as their ancestress, or, yet another possibility, according to Aristophanes, she was to be found in the underworld.[39]

Beings related to this deep, writhing force stood in direct, inseparable relation to the earthy, the dark, the dank, and the subterranean. Like the primordial being itself, their mark is one of bodily—as well as territorial—deviance and marginality. They hide away in remote places, in the farthest reaches of the Greek world, in zones of transgression, where the order of things comes undone, out past the edges of the human perspective. As if in exile in this wilderness on the borders of civilization, outside the poleis, these "beasts" seem to have been cast out far from the view of humans, in whom they arouse shuddering and dread, fear and disbelief.[40] Furthermore, these creatures of radical otherness usually dwell unseen, in dim places like caves, since the terror that the very sight of them instills is overwhelming.

The Attic tragedians' metaphorical portrayal of the Sphinx as a dog or a bitch (κύων) is also relevant here.[41] This may be alluding to Orthos's paternity. Above all, however, the understanding of the Sphinx is heard as an uncanny creature that, like the dog, is brought in connection with death. It is significant that, after Hesiod named the terrifying many-headed dog Cerberus Ἀΐδεω κύνα ("the dog of Hades"), an epigram from Thessaly dating from the fifth century BCE calls the Sphinx, whom Hesiod took as Cerberus's sister, Ἀΐδαο κύων ("the bitch of Hades"). As Manfred Lurker points out, the dog in Greek mythology is a creature of the liminal, marked by or inhabiting the threshold between this world and the next.[42] It is the animal escort of the Greek underworld goddess Hecate, and, as Cerberus, guards the entrance to Hades. In a few later representations—growing out of the attempts by Palaephatus and others to devise a rational explanation for the Greek myths about the gods, heroes, and monsters—the dog metaphor was taken literally and concretized into a physical description: now, instead of a lion's body, the Sphinx had the body of a dog.[43] In addition, the Sphinx is the marker of the threshold between life and death, between the world above and the world below, inasmuch as ancient popular belief outside the Oedipus myth (for example in vase painting) knows her as a demon of death, who snatches life away and who is present whenever a fatal danger threatens mankind.[44] Aeschylus' description of the Sphinx as a pestilential, "man-devouring Ker," is part of this general shift in her mythic characteristics.[45]

All of these conceptions connected with the Sphinx make it clear that the Greeks saw the threshold passage, which they associated with her, as a highly significant spatial and existential change. They conceived of it as a directional movement in both a horizontal and vertical direction. While the Sphinx's function as a bringer of death, as well as an escort into death, indicates a vertical movement between the world above and the underworld, her position in the vicinity of Thebes, even though it is in an elevated place on a mountain—Euripides called her οὔρειον τέρας ("mountain monster")[46]—implies, rather, a horizontal movement between city and wilderness. According to Pausanias' *Description of Greece*, she was to be found in the Kithara Mountains,[47] while Pseudo-Apollodorus's *Library* claims the Phikion Mountains (Φίκιον ὄρος) as her place of residence,[48] which, as Albin Lesky claimed,[49] should be linked to her original name Φίξ, as Hesiod mentions it.[50] Further corroboration is found in Lycophron's comparison of the seer Cassandra with the Phikion monster, the Φίκιον τέρας, in the *Alexandria*.[51] From Phikion there extended a plain all the way to Thebes,[52] one through which anyone hoping to enter the city had to pass, taking their chances with whatever awaited them. According to one variant in the tradition, the Sphinx posed her riddle to every traveler who passed her on the mountain on the way to or from Thebes. According to another, later tradition, she herself came daily to the marketplace of the city—which was, as we know, an especially significant zone in Greek antiquity[53]—so as to harvest her new victims there.[54] In every case, she dwelled in a "neutral zone" (van Gennep) outside of the seven mighty gates that marked Thebes as a defensive stronghold. Her existence represented a fatal insecurity for the Thebans, regardless of whether she appeared in a particular zone within the city or lurked in one of the zones on the outskirts.[55] Upon the mountain she is said to have devoured all those who failed to solve her riddle, wantonly grabbing one of the citizens and whisking him through the air. This zonal threat continued unchecked until her encounter with Oedipus, who stared down her menace and dread, solved her riddle, and brought her exploits to an end.

"Œdipe est double": Hero and Monster in Jean-Pierre Vernant

This encounter with the supernatural, in which the masculine and the feminine, the human and the bestial, the here and the hereafter, cross into one another, overlap and mix together, did not pass by Oedipus unnoticed. By no means did he cross through this mountainous wilderness at the edge of city, through this zone marked repeatedly as a threshold region by monsters and gates, without consequences. After all, according to van Gennep's and Turner's three-phase model, after his departure from Corinth, he found himself especially susceptible to the influence of unknown forces upon a journey through foreign lands, into the undefined threshold phase of general indeterminacy. In the confrontation with the Sphinx, Oedipus stepped, as it were, onto the threshold in order to transcend it and thus acquire a newly defined status, out of the "betwixt and between" state and into the urban culture of the polis. Thus was his fate similar to that of many other Greek heroes, before they could receive a throne, a country, a woman, or all of these together: like them, he had to prove himself in a particular test, so that by succeeding at "crossing the threshold" and "becoming a member of a new world," with all of its new rules and systems of order, he would finally consummate his pending change of state.[56] In this way, the Sphinx provides an extreme manifestation of the liminal phase's inherent danger, which the hero had to master, similar in this regard to other monsters, in which the Greeks beheld an existentially unstable mix of forms, a terrifying confusion that had to be overcome in order to establish or stabilize civilization and social order. This calls to mind the Gorgon Medusa, slain by Perseus,[57] the Chimaera, slain by Bellerophon,[58] and the Minotaur, slain by Theseus.[59]

In the encounter with the Sphinx, Oedipus both achieves and does not achieve a change in state of being; he both escapes and does not escape from the Sphinx. Only *externally* has he escaped the sphere of her power unimpaired. As depictions from the fifth century show, Oedipus stared at the Sphinx face-to-face, and in this frontality recognized the human quality ("man") within her liminal dimension of terror. Thus, the encounter has *internally* brought about a contact that leads to an exchange between a superhuman being and a human. For Oedipus, this means a one-way transmission into radical otherness. The numerous representations of the riddle scene that depict Oedipus and the Sphinx staring fixedly at one another make the following point: eye-to-eye, without averting the other's gaze, Oedipus is seized by what Sophocles describes as the "crooked-taloned oracle-singing Virgin" (γαμψώνυχα παρθένον χρησμῳδόν), from whose mouth the riddle darkly issued, just as from the mouth of a person seized by a god.[60] Oedipus may have shed light on the oracular darkness, which in Sophocles he claims before the seer Teiresias to be his special accomplishment (*OT* 390–400), by recalling how he came upon the riddle's solution—"man"—with intelligence and the power of understanding, yet in this encounter, head-to-head, something beyond the illuminating power of understanding happens: the "bitch," singing, usurped him and seized dominion from him.

This act of seizure by the threshold-being comes across in a dynamic of oppositional movements, which are stirred up by the passage through her zone. Since antiquity, researchers have tried to determine the nature of this dynamic, which Sophocles fruitfully shaped in *Oedipus the King*. In the twentieth century, there is the compelling work of Jean-Pierre Vernant,[61] a student of Gernet. In his essay "Ambiguïté et renversement: Sur la structure énigmatique d'Œdipe-roi" (1973), Vernant shows that an oppositional scheme of ambiguity and reversal underlies *Oedipus the King* in its language, style, plot, and conception of the protagonist, one that becomes especially clear in the figure of Oedipus, who unifies several oppositional moments in himself. "Oedipus is double. He is in himself a riddle whose meaning he can only guess when he discovers himself to be in every respect the op-posite of what he thought he was and appeared to be."[62] He can sur-mise the meaning of the riddle that he is. What Oedipus must discover is that he is in every sense—social, religious, and human—the very opposite of what he thought he was. The stranger from Corinth is a native citizen of Thebes, the riddle solver is himself a riddle, the guar-antor of justice is a deviant fiend, the seer of the light is blind, the sav-ior of the city is a harbinger of its doom, and the patron of civil cul-ture and society is actually unworthy of it. According to Vernant, these "ambiguities," in the sense of complementary schemes of opposition, constitute a continuous scheme of tragic construction, one which de-termines the development and presentation of the narrative. Here, positive values are wrapped in negative ones. Indeed, positive values prove themselves to be the very bearers of the negative.

The upshot of Vernant's remarks is to construct a comparison between the structure of tragedy and that of the scapegoat ritual, as it was consummated at the Athenian Thargelia festival. In the figure of the *pharmakos* (φαρμακός), Vernant recognizes the motif of the sac-rifice of the king, just as it also occurs in the sacrifice of the fool-king. He posits the thesis that the fundamental ambiguity of Oedipus—which in turn points to numerous subambiguities—encompasses the extremes of the god-king and the scapegoat, and that these two ex-tremes, when taken together, turn Oedipus into a riddle, as in a para-doxical formula with two distinct meanings: *"Divine king* and *pharma-kos*: These are the two sides to Oedipus that make a riddle of him by combining within him two figures, the one the reverse of the other, as in a formula with a double meaning."[63] The divine king, the savior of the city, the restorer of its order through the conquest of the Sphinx—this is one side of Oedipus. The other side is the way that he symbol-izes the *pharmakos*, the filth, deformity, madness, and crime, hence the malfunctioning of the social order that he embodies. As such, he is barred from the community and chased out beyond the city gates, so that evil—like the plague—may be banished from the given order and so that the transition from one state into another, better one may be facilitated.[64]

Whatever further conclusions we may draw from Vernant's re-

marks—whether it be that we recognize the scapegoat ritual in tragedy or that we merely see something of the scapegoat in the Oedipus
figure; whether, as suggested throughout, we recognize something of
this type in the Sphinx or even that we do not know how to deal with
these well-developed *pharmakos* analogies—the structure of ambiguity and reversal in *Oedipus the King*, as Vernant demonstrates, is hardly
debatable and is doubtlessly one reason for our ongoing fascination
with this tragedy right up until the present day. Furthermore, the analysis of Oedipus as a figure of ambiguity is plausible even without the
issue of the *pharmakos*—not least with regard to the encounter with
the Sphinx. The remarks on "ambiguity" and "reversal" not only illuminate the tragedy's revelations as they are represented on stage, in
which Oedipus so emphatically manifests the "duality of his being"
in speech and action,[65] but they also illuminate the parts of Oedipus'
life story that occur anterior to the staged events, especially the encounter that is of such great importance for the course of what is to
come. The reversal of positively valued experiences into the negative,
as analyzed by Vernant, lends Oedipus' story its character of salvation
and damnation. In and along with the Sphinx encounter, this reversal
obtains a particular kind of initiatory power. The confrontation with
this representative figure of hybridized duplicity initiates the hero,
in a sense, into his own inherently hybridized double nature. When
Oedipus confronts the Sphinx, staring at her head-on, bearing down
on her eyes so as to solve her riddle, he becomes the very Other that
she is. In a sort of exchange, the duplicity of the dark, oracular, sono-
rous, enigmatic riddle asker taps a vein of duplicity in the equally enigmatic riddle solver. The "fall" of the one posing the riddle at the end
of this encounter sets the mysterious reversal dynamic on an irrevers-
ible path, running up to Oedipus' "fall" at the tragedy's conclusion. All
positive values are now reversed into the negative: the hero solves the
riddle of the Sphinx with his formidable intellect, but not, however,
the riddle of his own existence. That is to say that he clears the way
for the very terror that brings death to the city. He does not therefore
stave off the actual blight, but rather unwittingly enables the fulfillment of his own blighted fate. By entering the sphere of the Sphinx,
he takes the decisive step toward fulfilling the prophecy—toward a

supposed "turning upward" and an actual "turning downward." Thus, the Sphinx's fall or plunge to her death, occasioned by the correct solution to her riddle, only apparently marks the ascent of the hero.[66] In reality, his own eventual turn toward downfall inheres in his triumphant upward turn upon solving the riddle: the supposedly upward movement of his accession to the throne is actually a move downward, encoded with his coming fall; his step "inward" to Thebes is actually the first step away, and the city's acceptance of the formerly expelled hero initiates his reexposure. As soon as Oedipus arrives in Thebes, fresh from his confrontation with the Sphinx, flushed with victory on account of his powers of understanding, and, accordingly, taken in as a hero and a ruler, he "falls," lacking insight into his own existence. He falls from the mountain through the gates of the city, "as far down as the valley" of hubris and blindness, where, in the end, his triumph will turn out to be wrapped in catastrophe and will prove to have been a step toward the triumph of a truly destructive fate. As he finally sees matters in the light of truth, recognizing his inner blindness, he blinds himself, "fallen" from the supreme height of the riddle solver, broken and ostracized. He thereby deprives himself of the eyes with which he first came into the transitional relationship with the enigmatic and the monstrous, recognizing it as his double. He removes the very eyes with which he lost himself in his double's gaze. The reaction of the Thebans makes clear the extent to which Oedipus now seems monstrous, he whom they had previously lauded as ἀνδρῶν δὲ πρῶτον, "the first among men," and as βροτῶν ἄριστ', "the best of the mortals" (OT 33, 46). There will be none on earth transformed into a more unfortunate state (ἀθλιώτερος) than Oedipus (OT 1204). The choir wails: εἴθε σ' εἴθ' [ἐγὼ] / μήποτ' εἰδόμαν ("If I'd, if I'd only / Never seen you" (OT 1217f.). And, with the words ὦ δεινὸν ἰδεῖν πάθος ἀνθρώποις, / ὦ δεινότατον πάντων ὅσ' ἐγὼ / προσέκυρσ' ἤδη ("O dreadful misery for humanity to see / O most dreadful of all / That my eyes have ever seen," OT 1297–1299), they turn their gaze away from him, he who also sees himself as κακός, "the doer of evil," as κάκιστον ἄνδρ', "the most depraved man" (OT 1397, 1433): φεῦ φεῦ, δύσταν'· ἀλλ' οὐδ' ἐσιδεῖν δύναμαί σε ("Woe, O miserable one! I cannot bear to look at you!"). Thus he awakes in them φρίκην: shuddering and terror (OT 1303f., 1306).

The story of the confrontation with the Sphinx can be read as the story of a man who refuses to engage with his own liminality. Cast out, adopted, and therefore liminal—and, furthermore, liminal as an adolescent—he enters a threshold state by setting off into the unknown. In this state, he first kills his father at the three-way intersection, a fundamentally liminal place insofar as it is a parting of the ways, a place where one must choose in which direction to go. Then he vanquishes a quintessentially liminal being, the Sphinx. To be sure, he accomplishes an outward change of state, but inwardly and finally, he remains in limbo and never comes to realize it. What seems to be a triumphant "royal initiation" for the one who overcame the Sphinx through the strength of his intellect is, as it were, an initiation through a δίμορφον θηρίον into a threshold state as a δίμορφον θηρίον—into the state of being a real "threshold foot" (Schwell-Fuß), just as the mark of his swollen foot signifies. A parodic depiction of the riddle scene on an *oinochoe*, dated from 450/440 BCE, also seems to have made reference to this.[67] This Boeotian jug not only depicts the Sphinx as an exceedingly repellent chimaera—with her sharp, pointed head, giant beard and ears, and lizard's tail—but also the hero, who has the lower body (legs and tail) of a dog, κύων, and supports himself on two spears, which are made to look almost like two makeshift extra limbs. The constellation of Oedipus before the Sphinx appears here as a constellation of two beings of extreme liminality: one κύων before another κύων, one monster before another.

This contemptuous, disparaging depiction of the same riddle scene that was so common in the vase painting of the time, in which Oedipus usually appears as a man of intelligence, almost perfectly touches on the problematic of the hero's history. After answering the riddle with "man," he does not comport himself in a way appropriate to the values of his culture, but rather more like a hybrid being from the family of the monsters that Hesiod mentions in *Theogony*, monsters of the Echidna line, which includes incest. Since he begets in his mother what Seneca calls an *impius fetus* ("wicked progeny") and produces *fratres sibi* ("brothers of himself"), he becomes an *implicitum malum*, a "muddled evil," an abomination even more convoluted than the Sphinx: *magisque monstrum Sphinge perplexum sua*.[68] Aside from ritual exceptions, for example within the Pharaoh's family in ancient Egypt, there is no known ancient society in which sexual intercourse between close blood relatives was not an absolute and highly punishable taboo. And yet Oedipus ignores this age-old prohibition. In doing so, he abrogates the natural order of the generations and perverts human existence.[69] Admittedly, when considering van Gennep's theory of material threshold markers, he appears to have successfully completed his transition into a new state by entering through the city gates of Thebes, that is, with his spatial crossing of the threshold (*marge*), and then with his successful intercourse with the queen. But since the queen is and has always been his mother, he has actually succeeded only in destroying the social order and making himself into the very source of the danger that lurks within the threshold state, one that the citizens of Thebes must ward off. He first becomes cognizant of his liminality when he solves the riddle surrounding Laius' murder and his actual heritage; and as Sophocles so potently represents it, recognizes himself as a monster, coming to understand that man cannot determine his own nature, but rather that his nature is assigned to him by superhuman entities, in this case by Apollo speaking through the oracle. There are two consequences to be acknowledged: first, regarding the demand that was articulated by Creon as Apollo's decree, and then also by Oedipus himself and by Teiresias, that he must request permission to leave the city;[70] and second, that he must express his wish to cast himself out onto the mountain, outside of the city's culture, where he had already been cast out once as a child.[71] The final nested commandment (reversal) thereby fulfills his original destiny.[72] In this way, Oedipus expresses his submission to his own liminality. Since he has only superficially left behind the life of the castaway inside Thebes and all the norms that prevail there, he sees at last the only form of existence appropriate to what he really is: a sojourn beyond the borders of Thebes, in quasi-monstrous wilderness, just like the Sphinx, his double, before him.

Regarded from this perspective, the formula that the Sphinx episode suggests — a formula that also underscores the meaning of the encounter for the rest of Sophocles' tragedy — is as follows: "No passage before the Sphinx, no catastrophe; no catastrophe, no self-realization."

It is not without reason that the many contributors to the Oedipus myth contrived an encounter with the Sphinx. Indeed, the Sphinx is among the most suited of all figures in antique mythology for the task of illustrating liminality. It is hard to imagine any figure standing as a more compelling marker of the "betwixt and between" state, as the Oedipus myth develops it. No other figure could bring the many thresholds (occidental/oriental, Egyptian/Greek, human/animal, masculine/feminine) to bear so impressively and so multifariously. It is no wonder, then, that the scene of Oedipus before the Sphinx has given scholars so many riddles to ponder and, from antiquity up through the centuries, has been taken up and interpreted in the most varied ways possible by artists, poets, and thinkers. The constellation of these two figures is a figuration of unparalleled indeterminacy and ambiguity. In light of the great number of depictions in vase painting in the fifth century BCE, it is conceivable that artists at that time had already moved beyond a consistently and purely positive conception of Oedipus as a representative of autonomous intelligence and cultural progress, toward redefining his story as a cautionary tale of human hubris. This is similar to the Attic tragedians, whose influence and impact on the vase painting of the time is beyond question.[73] The image of Oedipus before the Sphinx, the hero face-to-face with the Other who is his double, is in this sense not only a testament about or for autonomous intelligence, but also a pictorial warning against the fall of man into an existence as a δίμορφον θηρίον, into which it is always possible to mutate. In the end, what Sophocles' version strikingly and unforgettably expresses is a limitation of an excessive faith in human powers of understanding, for intellectual superiority is in no way able to preserve the hero against error, hubris, and blindness.

PART TWO

Oedipus before the Sphinx in Modernity:
On Freud and Cocteau

✧

CHAPTER THREE

Freud the Riddle Solver
and the "Riddle of the Feminine"

The powerful constellation of Oedipus and the Sphinx experienced re-newed attention in the late nineteenth and early twentieth centuries, as art, poetry, and not least psychology took up ancient myths to portray and discourse upon the relations between the sexes. Like other figures of ancient mythology, Oedipus and the Sphinx now found themselves deployed in many iconographic and literary contexts and, integrated into theory, were transposed into conceptual ideas, with encoding at times unaltered and at other times adapted to particular theses.

As scholars have shown, one characteristic feature of this recourse to mythology and its conceptual realignment is its generally retrogres-sive quality: It took place in the throes of the gender conflict that was ever present in literature, art, and scholarship between 1850 and 1930.[1] By means of various narratives and transplanted fragments of ancient mythology, its aim was to articulate, from a masculine perspective, no-tions of the enigmatic and overwhelmingly sensual nature of woman, and thereby avert the dangers that seemed to emanate from her. Such depictions of the Sphinx, like those of other female figures of Greco-Roman mythology (e.g., Circe, the Sirens, the Naiads, the Maenads), particularly as idealized images of a hypertrophic sexuality, are fairly unmistakable reflections of the restrictive sexual codex of the patriarchal, bourgeois society of Sigmund Freud's own day, which was subjected to critical analysis in his writings.[2]

It has often been observed, justly in my view, that Freud's criticism was hardly supportive of female liberation movements and their concepts, which had started to emerge in the nineteenth century. His assumptions about femininity, sexual development, and female sexuality have provoked trenchant objections since the 1920s and 1930s, especially from female psychoanalysts like Karen Horney, one of the first critics of Freud's views on feminine psychology, and Melanie Klein, who brought considerable insight into the field of psychoanalysis by highlighting the perspective of the mother.[3] More recently, and since the late 1970s, such criticism has grown more vociferous within the context of feminist discussions.[4] Many theorists base their work on Simone de Beauvoir's critique of Freud, who is here regarded as having taken the value of virility. Accordingly, de Beauvoir takes Freud to task for not considering the social origins of masculine and paternal power and privilege.[5] In these discussions, the self-image of the psychoanalyst, attained through the association of science with recourse to myth, runs into particular criticism. Moreover, and inextricably linked to this, reference is made to the fatal consequences for the redefinition of gender roles that around 1900 was long overdue, given Freud's considerable contribution to the remythification of these roles in creating a myth of femininity. In this myth, which has been much discussed in writings on gender concerns since the 1970s, femininity is inseparably linked to enigma.[6]

The words with which Freud addressed his (fictitious) readership in his *New Series of Lectures* on *The Introduction to Psychoanalysis* (1933) are particularly significant in regard to this remythification:

> Throughout history people have knocked their heads against the riddle of the nature of femininity [. . .]. Nor will you have escaped worrying over this problem—those of you who are men; to those of you who are women this will not apply—you are yourselves the problem.[7]

It seems that Freud either did not consider the possibility that women could be intellectually active themselves in solving riddles or that he regarded it as an indication of "inferiority," a reaction to an organic "defect," *viz.* the absence of a penis—in other words, as a form of "penis-envy."[8] Assuming the male body to be the normative point of reference, his analyses, wherever he found female intellectual activity, regarded such activity as an appropriation of "male" qualities and "the wish to get the longed-for penis."[9] By thus excluding woman from solving riddles and reducing her to a riddle in her own right, unable to solve herself but soluble to him by psychoanalytical methods, he was styling himself—as scholars have sufficiently shown[10]—as a solver of riddles and subjugator of Sphinxes all in one—in other words, as a modern Oedipus.

This is not the place to trace in detail the various studies on these matters or to describe comprehensively the remythifying aspects of Freud's reinterpretation of the Oedipus myth. It will suffice to make brief reference to elements of this reinterpretation that are illuminating in respect to an understanding of Cocteau—not least because Cocteau often commented on Freud. I will now outline the concept of the Oedipus complex, by which Freud hoped to understand attachment to a developmental phase of early childhood characterized by libidinous attraction to the mother and rivalry with the father, and the significance of the Oedipus-Sphinx constellation for Freud's work.

Infantile and Juvenile Wish Fulfillment: Freud as κράτιστος ἀνήρ

Freud introduced the concept of the Oedipus complex in 1900 in his *Traumdeutung* (*Interpretation of Dreams*), a work in which—and this too is of interest in relation to Cocteau—he sought to overcome the opposition of dream and reality. To speak with Foucault, dream no longer constituted a "non-sense" for the rational mind, but the "sense" of the subconscious, which could be decoded through knowledge.[11] In the spirit of this "sense," the ancient myth is interpreted as the fulfillment of a "primitive wish of our childhood," so that the Oedipus figure is reduced to parricidal and incestuous urges respectively directed at the father and focused on the mother—urges that Freud argues to be deeply rooted in the human soul:

> His [sc. Oedipus'] fate moves us only because it could have been our own as well, because at our birth the oracle pronounced the same

curse upon us as it did on him. It was perhaps ordained that we should all of us turn our first sexual impulses towards our mother, our first hatred and violent wishes against our father. Our dreams convince us of it. King Oedipus, who killed his father Laius and married his mother Jocasta, is only the fulfillment of our childhood wish. But, more fortunate than he, we have since succeeded, at least insofar as we have not become psychoneurotics, in detaching our sexual impulses from our mothers, and forgetting our jealousy of our fathers. We recoil from the figure who has fulfilled that ancient childhood wish with the entire sum of the repression which these wishes have since undergone within us.[12]

Freud's abundant use of the first person plural forms of the personal and possessive pronouns ("we [. . .] all," "we," "our") shows that he saw the infantile Oedipal conflict (and the trouble that arises when the adult remains trapped in the nexus of that conflict) as an anthropological constant. A letter he wrote to Wilhelm Fliess indicates the same intent. Freud wrote this letter three years before the *Traumdeutung*, in the same year that he subjected himself to a thorough self-analysis. Referring to the feelings toward his parents that he observed in himself, he here for the first time makes reference in his psychological work to Sophocles' *Oedipus the King*, a text that was familiar to him from his school days in the humanities program at the *Gymnasium*.[13] He attributes the gripping power of the drama to the universality of the experience undergone by the character in the play:

I have found, in my own case too, [the phenomenon of] being in love with my mother and jealous of my father, and I now consider it a universal event in early childhood [. . .]. If this is so, we can understand the gripping power of Oedipus Rex, in spite of all the objections that reason raises against the presupposition of fate [. . .]. [. . .] [T]he Greek legend seizes upon a compulsion which everyone recognizes because he senses its existence within himself. Everyone in the audience was once a budding Oedipus in fantasy and each recoils in horror from the dream fulfillment here transplanted into reality, with the full quantity of repression which separates his infantile state from his present one.[14]

The extent of Freud's identification with Oedipus, not only during the period of his self-analysis but throughout his life, is apparent from the many occasions on which he defined himself as Oedipus. We recall the epithet "Antigone" that he attached to his daughter Anna when he contracted cancer: "Anna-Antigone," the indispensable colleague, secretary, assistant, agent, nurse during his illness, representative at conferences. The sobriquet indicates that he identified Anna with the faithful daughter of Oedipus and himself with the latter.[15] This very constellation (father-daughter) already shows that Freud's enduring interest in Oedipus went beyond the complex of "primitive wishes" of childhood that he had discovered in himself, that the Theban figure offered far greater scope for personal identification.

The relevance of the Theban but also the Egyptian Sphinx for Freud makes this "far greater scope" particularly apparent.[16] An obsessive collector of antiquities—especially small Egyptian, Greek, and Roman statues, many of which filled his consultation room and covered his desk—Freud had several pieces depicting the Sphinx.[17] The most famous one is the Greek terracotta figure of the Theban Sphinx which decorated Freud's study in London. Equally well known is the large print of the Egyptian Sphinx at Giza in his front room at 20 Maresfield Gardens.[18] In view of his identification with Oedipus, two modern pictorial adaptations of the Theban configuration are particularly revealing, insofar as they crop up in places or at times of special significance in Freud's life and work: first, the reproduction of *Oedipus and the Sphinx*, a painting by Jean Auguste Dominique Ingres (1808); and second, a portrait medallion of Freud himself by the Viennese sculptor and medalist Carl Maria Schwerdtner (1906). The framed print of Ingres's famous painting hung in the analyst's treatment room at Berggasse 19 in Vienna, where Freud lived and worked from 1881 to 1938. Here, of course, is where his *Traumdeutung* and other works originated and where his case studies took place (fig. 2). The analysand who approached Freud's coach saw Ingres's painting just to the right, at the foot of the couch. Schwerdtner's medallion, which has a bas-relief of Freud in profile on the obverse and a copy of a Greek depiction of Oedipus before the Sphinx on the reverse, was commissioned for Freud by friends and colleagues in 1906 to celebrate his fiftieth birthday and was presented to him on that occasion (fig. 3).

FIG. 2. Berggasse 19, Freud's consulting room, detailed view of the end of the couch, including reproduction of Ingres's *Oedipus and the Sphinx* (*Œdipe et le Sphinx*). Photograph taken by Edmund Engelmann in 1938 before Freud left Vienna after the Nazi annexation of Austria. Reproduced courtesy of Todd Engelmann and Freud Museum, London.

Avers   Revers

FIG. 3. Medallion for the fiftieth birthday of Sigmund Freud, 1906, by Carl Maria Schwerdtner, which shows Oedipus and the Sphinx. Its inscription is from Sophocles' *Oedipus the King*: "he who unraveled the great riddle, and was first in power." Bronze, 60 mm, Archives of the University of Vienna, Inv. 102.2.7.

In the Ingres painting, the original of which hangs in the Louvre (fig. 4), it is striking that the positioning of the two figures with the Sphinx above and the attributes of Oedipus as traveler are taken from the portrayal of the constellation that the fifth-century BCE vase painters made canonical. It depicts a winged Sphinx, with a lion's body and a woman's head and breasts, sitting high upon a rock. Before the creature we see a pensive Oedipus, almost naked, his spears, hat, and cloak visible to his right in the background. This portrayal of the mythical constellation admits many interpretations. For instance, it can be read as reflecting the relationship between the sexes. At the center of the image, aglow with color as if illuminated, stands Oedipus, one arm crooked, supporting himself with one foot up on the rock of the Sphinx in front of him, facing her with a thoughtful expression on his face, but not looking her in the eye. With his left hand he indicates the Sphinx, with his right hand, himself. The scene is sexualized by the fact that Oedipus and the Sphinx do not face each other at eye level but rather "forehead to breasts." The accent is thus placed on Oedipus' intellectual capacity, while in his counterpart it is the secondary—corporeal—gender characteristics and their erotic signal functions that are highlighted. The gaze of the viewer is also drawn toward the prominent swell of the Sphinx's breasts, because the composition of the picture puts them on the same axis as the head of the pensive hero

FIG. 4. J. A. D. Ingres, *Œdipe et le Sphinx*, 1808–1825, oil on canvas, 189 × 144 cm, Musée du Louvre, Paris. Ingres first painted this composition in 1808, then changed it before presenting it at the Salon of 1827.

in the center of the scene. Moreover, whereas the head of the Sphinx and the rest of her body are in shadow, her breasts are bathed in light like Oedipus.

The presence of this reproduction hanging in Freud's workrooms is made all the more significant by the fact that the Sphinx and a pensive Oedipus also appear in similar positions, likewise modeled on the Greek composition, on the medallion made for Freud's fiftieth birthday. The medallion bears an inscription in ancient Greek asserting that the pictured hero is a "riddle solver," superior in strength and power to all men. The quotation is from line 1525 of *Oedipus the King*, ὅς τὰ κλείν' αἰνίγματ' ἤδει καὶ κράτιστος ἦν ἀνήρ ("he who unraveled the great riddle, and was a most powerful man").[19] It is particularly telling that versions of this picture were reproduced in a bookplate designed for Freud in 1910, and that the Oedipus-Sphinx constellation further served as the logo of the Internationaler Psychoanalytischer Verlag (IPV).[20] The personal bookplate, a lithograph (by Bertold Löffler) based on the medallion, also displayed line 1525 of *Oedipus the King*. The logo of the IPV iconographically draws on Ingres's painting.[21] As Richard H. Armstrong has argued convincingly, the repeated deployment of the Oedipus-Sphinx configuration was due to the psychoanalytical movement's intention to establish it as their icon honoring Freud, the founder of the movement, as chief riddle solver and most powerful man.[22]

Particularly revealing in terms of how important the Oedipus-Sphinx configuration was to Freud himself is the anecdote told in relation to the presentation of the medallion. Freud's pupil Ernest Jones tells us that Freud was deeply moved when he saw the medallion and glanced at the inscription. According to Jones, Freud became pale, as if he had seen a ghost, and at last admitted to the gathering why the words moved him so deeply. As a young student, Freud confessed, he once strolled around the great court of the University of Vienna, studying the busts of former professors there, and "had the phantasy [. . .] of seeing his own bust [. . .] inscribed with the *identical* words he now saw on the medallion."[23] Jones finishes his account by commenting that he himself ensured that this dream of the young Freud was fulfilled, albeit posthumously (on 4 February 1955). This event may have been an incidence of wish-fulfillment from Freud's childhood and youth.

More could be said about these portrayals of Oedipus before the Sphinx, for instance concerning the size and positioning of the Ingres reproduction in Freud's room or the anecdotal and parabolic qualities of the story woven around the gift of the medallion. But it will here suffice to stress the indicative significance of the portrayals. Both images attest to the identificatory potential inherent, for Freud, in

Oedipus' function as the solver of riddles, especially when read in the context of Freud's recorded remarks on the presentation of the medallion. The analyst regarded himself to be exceptional, not average—not simply a man who had gone through the Oedipal conflict of childhood like any other ἀνήρ, but rather a riddle solver of mythical dimensions: as the Greek formulation κράτιστος intimates, a superlative hero.[24]

In view of the human quest for excellence in performance, which manifests itself in sometimes remarkable ways in the thoughts and actions of competitive personalities, such an identification would be neither surprising nor particularly tenuous. However, in light of Freud's deficit perspective in respect of women, this identification is altogether striking. As can be seen, for instance, in the passage cited above from the *Introductory Lectures*, Freud not "only" declared the human subconscious in general to be feminine, but also called woman herself a riddle and feminine sexuality the "dark continent."[25] In spite of the inadequacy of his knowledge of femininity and feminine sexuality that he admits here, he formulated assumptions that allow no doubt of the "inferiority" of woman on the one hand and his own analytical competence and the efficacy of his methods and insights on the other. In this way, he affirmed his view of himself in his sexual and professional identity explicitly at the expense of woman. In the words of Inge Stephan, he "displaced" the "riddle question of the Sphinx" from man to woman, which, as Ingres's portrayal insinuates, left her intellectually diminished, while the man—and of all men, the κράτιστος ἀνήρ, Freud himself—was endowed with a victorious analytical mind.

Perversion and Hubris:
Thoughts on the Anecdote of Freud's "Turning Pale"

A blunt deduction may be made here: Although Freud's self-analysis constituted a far better approximation of the ancient demand for self-knowledge than the blind rush to incest of his ancient "predecessor,"[26] and although it may even have heralded an epoch-making turn in consciousness as an answer to the riddle of the Sphinx (i.e., the subconscious), Freud remained blind to what he himself called the "riddle of femininity";[27] and his intellect, like that of the Greek Oedipus, did not prevent him from interpreting human existence in a reactionary way or from perverting it in regard to woman. This perversion was not the face-value act of perversion with the mother, but something much more subtle: he conducted a "scientific," "systematic" subversion of the process, then ongoing, to achieve parity in relations between the genders, and by doing so, he perverted it.

Although Freud certainly did not diagnose this form of perversion of human existence in himself, it is conceivable that, if we lend credence to Jones's anecdotal account, he turned pale when he read the inscription for another reason, apart from (or in addition to) the fantasy of renown that he confessed in recalling his youthful aspirations. It may be that in this moment, faced with the Oedipus-Sphinx constellation, he glimpsed himself for the first time not in the sense of his own reinterpretation of the Oedipus myth, but in the sense of the admonitions of the ancient Attic tragedians, who assessed the "ascent" of man while simultaneously warning of the freedom gained and the possibility of hubris and "fall."

The possibility that this was the reason why Freud turned pale is reinforced by the fact that he knew the context of the Sophocles quotation concerned. He had quoted it himself in the *Traumdeutung*:

> The contrast with which the chorus takes its leave: ". . . Behold, this was Oedipus, / Greatest of men; he held the key to the deepest mysteries; / Was envied by all his fellow-men for his great prosperity; / Behold, what a full tide of misfortune swept over his head [Soph. *OT* 1524ff.]"[28]—this admonition refers to us too and our pride, who have grown so wise and powerful in our own estimation since our childish years. Like Oedipus we live in ignorance of those wishes, offensive to morality and forced upon us by Nature, and once they have been revealed, there is little doubt we would all rather turn our gaze away from the scenes of our childhood.[29]

So Freud may have been aware of the difficulty associated with the κράτιστος ἀνήρ attribution on the medallion. As his remark indicates ("The contrast with which the chorus takes its leave"), the Sophocles quotation comes from the famous final chorus of the tragedy, whose "opposition" of Oedipus as powerful riddle solver on the one hand and one sunk in the "full tide of misfortune" on the other resounds as a farewell to the once mighty king, and reminds us that we should praise no human life before it ends.[30] In this context, we see the *decontextualized* paean to a man at the height of his powers on the medallion *recontextualized* as a farewell to one who has suffered a tragic fall. Or, to put it another way, the mythical dynamic that determines Oedipus' fate shines through: a dynamic of contrary currents, in which the hero's ascent contains the seed of his fall, his triumph his downfall.

It is conceivable, then, that Freud was overcome by an intimation of hubris and by the fear that the mythical dynamic whereby positive values turn negative might run its course after all. This seems all the more plausible given his conviction that he was a "better" modern Oedipus who had averted the fate of the ancient hero through rational analytical power (as though achieved by φαίνειν, that is, by bringing light into the darkness of a case by analysis, by illuminating his own issue and those of his patients).[31] As the cited excerpt from the *Traumdeutung* shows, he had even understood the admonition of the final chorus (that a life should be judged for value and coherence only at its end) as supporting his view ("legendary matter which corroborates the belief"), that "being in love with one parent and hating the other" happen in the souls of almost all children, and "belong to the indispensable stock of psychical impulses" that develop in infancy and are so important in the pathology of later neurosis.[32] He took the final chorus as a call not to live "in ignorance of those wishes, offensive to morality and forced upon us b Nature," but to face up to the "scenes from our childhood" for the sake of "revealing" those wishes.[33] Perhaps, in the very moment that the medallion was presented (as he gazed at the constellation of Oedipus and the Sphinx), he suddenly saw the reality of Sophocles' warning—that intellectual superiority is no defense against error, hubris, or blindness, and that man—indeed, by reason of his powers of analytical understanding, thinking himself a victorious "solver of riddles" and "conqueror of the Sphinx"—is capable at any moment of perverting his existence and regressing to a δίμορφον θηρίον.

Ultimately, though, Freud was certainly not guilty of pusillanimity or self-doubt when it came to his appraisal of his own achievement, as his well-known self-contextualization in scholarly history shows. According to his own assessment, human conceit has suffered three great reversals. The first was inflicted by Copernicus, who tore the Earth out of its position at the center of the universe. Then came Darwin, whose work spelled the end of human "arrogance," of man's belief in himself as a creature with an immortal soul and of divine descent, quite separate from the world of animals. The third reversal, the "most wounding," was the psychological one, dealt by psychoanalysis, that is, by Freud himself, who had shown mankind that "the life of our sexual instincts cannot be wholly tamed"—a discovery that, according to Freud, amounts to the statement that "the ego is not master in its own house."[34]

CHAPTER FOUR

"The night that concerns me is different"
Cocteau's Distancing from Freud

Regardless of whatever really happened when Freud received his medallion on his fiftieth birthday—whether he blanched for the reason suggested above, or for another reason, or not at all—Jean Cocteau would probably have advanced the opinion that Freud well deserved to grow pale. Cocteau was no admirer of Freud and repeatedly spoke out against his "art of interpretation."[1] To the claim that this "art" was in principle applicable to all productions of the human imagination, Cocteau responded with unbridled contempt, dismissing it quite simply as a sexual obsession on Freud's part as well as an attempt to detect his own "sickness" in his patients. Cocteau explained the success of what he termed Freud's "naïve key of dreams," which made a complex of the simplest dream, by its resonance with an idle, decadent society in which everything revolved around sex.[2]

It is certainly no overinterpretation to understand Cocteau's work—inter alia—as a repudiation of Freud and particularly of Freud's *Traumdeutung*, precisely because that work contains elements of dream that provoke psychoanalytical interpretation and prove equal to it. Many of Cocteau's statements support such a view, both contemptuous remarks about Freud and comments on his own understanding of dream. Cocteau does concede that Freud is right to say that an artist need not be consciously aware of particular things for those things to become subsequently crucial elements of his work.[3] He also agrees that the artist is not responsible for what emerges into a film from his shadows and his unconscious mind, and that these things can be discovered only by those who judge the artist.[4] Elsewhere, however, he turns against Freud, explicitly and implicitly. Regarding Freud's research methods and their results, he describes them as mediocre, vulgar, and poor.[5] More seriously, he accuses Freud of exploiting patients for his own purposes, of reducing the patient to the norm of the majority.[6] Cocteau repeatedly explains his own attitude to dreams and points to the openness of his own work, in order to distance himself from the claims to absolute validity and understanding inherent in Freud's dream analysis. He similarly sets himself apart from the views of many other contemporary artists who concerned themselves with dreams as well as from recipients of his own work who took an analytical approach.[7] He cites the proliferation of interpretations of his works already apparent in his own day and protests against the attempt to overdetermine with meaning things that were intentionally not to be comprehended. This standpoint is distilled into the programmatic formula from Cocteau's *Démarche d'un poète*: "The demon of understanding. It is without doubt the original sin in the paradise of art."[8] Analogous statements are found elsewhere, for example, in "La poésie au cinématographe":

NB

> The compulsion to understand—whereas the world in which people live and the acts of God appear to be incoherent, contradictory, and incomprehensible—the compulsion to understand, I say, shuts off all those grand and exquisite feelings that art unfolds in those solitudes where man no longer seeks to understand but to feel.[9]

Between Finding and Invention: "Archaeology" as a Shared Figure of Thought in Freud and Cocteau

Cocteau's unbending attitude toward Freud and (psycho)analytical ambitions in general is understandable given that, while they had similar views of dream as potential for an enormous extension of human epistemological possibility, the aims of their respective interests were diametrically opposed. Freud's aim is hermeneutic, the deciphering of the meaning of the unconscious, "spelling out" the dream and transposing it to the realm of knowledge and epistemology. His purpose is to acquire validated insights. Cocteau, meanwhile, works on the assumption that a narrow recourse to "logic" restricts the perceptive capacities of the individual. Contrary to the "iconoclastic principle of psychoanalysis,"[10] he strives to write in images, thereby questioning language as an instrument of meaning and knowledge and repudiating all efforts at scientific understanding. He is interested neither in systematic procedures aimed at classificatory definition, categorization, and ordering—including systematic oneirocriticism—nor in taming the influence of the subconscious by trying to make it comprehensible. Rather, he hopes to dissolve stable structures and terminologies of order both in his own creative process and in the reception of his work. In this regard, he coincides with his contemporary Theodor W. Adorno, who in an aphorism of 1946–1947 claimed that, "the task of art today is to bring chaos into order."[11]

Freud, conversely, wants to bring order into chaos. He studies the subconscious out of interest for the conscious mind, which he values as a higher authority; and in this context he considers the interpretation of dreams the "via regia"[12] to an understanding of the phenomena taking place in the subconscious. Analysis enables him to identify the latent "dream thought" behind the manifest "dream content"—to solve the dream. He thinks of the dream content as a process of thinking in images that is distorted by the "dream work" and must be translated back by free association, by inserting a syllable or a word for each image. Thus, the enigmatic image is dissolved by means of verbal, linear unfolding. Freud's explicative division of dream formation into two phases—first, the constitution of the "dream thoughts" belonging to the (as yet) unconscious process of thinking; and second the "dream work," responsible for the transformation of the dream thought into "dream content"—allows him to strip the dream of its "fantastic character" (*phantastisches Gepräge*).[13]

It is precisely such a "fantastic character" that marks out most of Cocteau's work, and deliberately so. To some extent, Cocteau "simulates" dream, translating its "living language" into the manifest world to create a dream analogy ("Langue vivante du rêve. Langue morte du réveil . . . Il faut interpréter, traduire"—"Living language of the dream. Dead language of awakening . . . One must interpret, one must translate").[14] Cocteau aims to disengage the light of the conscious mind, to undermine intellectual constructions, in order to yield to the nightside of the soul and create in a state of blindness, with the hope, constantly dashed, that his audience will adopt a similar approach in receiving his work.[15] Whatever his "dark self" (*moi obscur*)[16] or "nocturnal self" (*moi nocturne*)[17] conveys to him must be accepted as a sleeper accepts the dream.[18] He must then bring it to the visible "light" of consciousness by a dreamlike language, interwoven with motifs of a state of consciousness that has detached itself from "objective" reality, putting it before the eyes of his audience in an almost acrobatic feat of illusionism. To Cocteau, this is the real work of an archaeologist: the "véritable travail d'archéologue."[19] Thus, in the foreword to the book edition of the *Testament d'Orphée*, he calls himself an "archaeologist of [his] night"—"archéologue de ma nuit."[20]

"Archaeology" is also one of Freud's favored figures of thought. He used the analogy repeatedly from the 1890s to the late 1930s in describing the methods of his new science, and it has attracted much notice in scholarship, especially over the past three decades.[21] This figure of thought warrants a brief examination here. As the *tertium comparationis*, it clearly shows where Freud's and Cocteau's views of dream coincided and differed.

Freud and Cocteau assumed the existence of an unconscious reservoir in the psyche that fascinated both of them as "archaeologists of the interior." However, the positions they adopted in relation to this storehouse differed, as did their respective "archaeological" approaches. To a certain extent, Freud saw rationality as the grand, ultimate destination of individual and collective development, and deployed the "god *Logos*," whom he invoked in 1927 in *The Future of an Illusion*, against a regression into mythic narratives.[22] He argues here as a scientist proceeding in a systematic way, employing archaeological practice in relation to (and for the benefit of) hermeneutic or psychoanalytical methodology, so as to counter the seductive power of illusions of which he believed science should be free. In contrast, Cocteau was unwilling to be limited by the boundaries of the rational and wished instead to dissolve them. He thus considered mythical narratives to be *filles de l'invisible,*[23] "daughters of the invisible," to whom he hoped to draw near. He saw himself—and made his artistic statements—in the spirit of the *moi obscur*, making an analogy between archaeological work as a process that oscillates between finding and invention, and poetic creativity as the retrieval of poetic treasures from the "internal night."

Cocteau, then, distanced himself clearly from Freud's high-profile "excavations." He recoiled from the analytical fathoming of the night with the aid of the scientific discipline of "archaeology." Freud, who even in 1895 was already seeing the "technique of excavating a buried city" and "clearing away the pathogenic psychical material layer by layer" as equivalent procedures,[24] incorporated actual archaeological objects from his art collection into the therapeutic process.[25] He illustrated results of psychoanalytical work with archaeological comparisons, and made an analogy, apparent for instance in the treatise (which Cocteau knew) "Delusions and Dreams in Jensen's 'Gradiva'" (1907),[26] between the work of psychoanalysis and a poetic process that invoked the "science of the ancients." Cocteau shared this relation to antiquity. He too made the ancient usable for the present. But the "archaeological" claim of Freud as discoverer and *reconstructor* of childhood propensities of an individual's life history seemed suspect to him. Instead, Cocteau regarded himself more as a "craftsman" and *deconstructor* whose aim was to transcend the everyday and the visible world. He countered Freud's endeavor "to bring light into the darkness" with his own initiatives "to bring night into day"—which, to him, meant creating works that "belong to the night in plain day," "born of the marriage of the conscious and the unconscious"—"née des noces du conscient et de l'inconscient."[27] Cocteau was concerned with making works express an adjacency and coexistence of day and night, conscious and unconscious, by translating that which wells up from the depths of the *moi obscure* into a *clair-obscur* as in a dream, hence blurring the boundaries of space and time. In a conversation with André Fraigneau, he explained that his concern was to discover and recover the oeuvre pre-existing in himself: "It is from our reserve, from our night, that things come to us. Our work pre-exists within us. The problem consists in *discovering* it (*invenire*). We are but its archaeologists."[28]

The existence of a spiritual component in the dream aesthetic should not be overlooked. Cocteau saw the individual unconscious as an aspect of a universal, abyssal night, and himself as the *poète* in its service. To give himself up to it and dive in meant opening himself reverentially and humbly to a transcendental truth—behind the visible world—to something "more true than the truth" ("plus vrai que le vrai"):[29] "The poet receives orders from a night that the ages accumulate in his person [. . .] of which he is but the humble vehicle" ("le poète reçoit des ordres [. . .] d'une nuit que les siècles accumulent en sa personne, [. . .] dont il n'est que l'humble véhicule").[30] In his eyes, poetry was intrinsically always—in an abstract sense of simple transcendence—"religious."[31]

From this perspective of longing for transpersonal dissolution, Cocteau saw Freud's psychoanalytical approach, in which religion is regarded as an expression of underlying psychological neuroses and distress, as reductionist and limited. Freud's biography could shed some light on the psychoanalyst's opinion. Born to Jewish parents in the Roman Catholic town of Freiberg, Moravia, Freud attempted throughout his life to understand religion from a critical perspective. A departure point for this endeavor was Ludwig Feuerbach's theory that God is a projection of the unconscious mind. Convinced that religion was a great hindrance to society that could be set aside in favor of reason and science, Freud wanted to prove that religion is merely an illusion, based on the infantile need for a powerful father figure. Thus he wrote several papers and books that provided a psychological foundation to the Feuerbachian idea that the essence of religion is human nature ("theology as anthropology"). Especially noteworthy are Freud's essays explicitly devoted to religious themes: *Obsessive Actions and Religious Practices* (1907), *Totem and Taboo* (1913), *The Future of an Illusion* (1927), *Civilization and Its Discontents* (1930), and *Moses and Monotheism* (1938). The views that Freud presents across these works are in no way consistent, each one guided by different goals and relating to diverse areas of research in religious studies. All the same, one can discern dominant themes, such as the suggestions that religion is an attempt to control the Oedipal complex, a means of wish fulfillment, an infantile delusion, or an attempt to control the outside world.[32]

For Cocteau, Freud's approach should be considered an expression of rational despair. From the highly dismissive remarks about psychoanalysis scattered across Cocteau's works, it becomes clear that he accused Freud of attributing everything to a sexuality that is limited to the sphere of the individual and thereby reducing everything that transcends everyday consciousness to the unconscious. In Cocteau's view, Freud tendentiously and simplistically interprets the emergence of anything transcendental and "higher" as an irruption of something "lower," and by this means, he confirms himself as a scientist at the expense of his analytical subjects.

This assessment is most clearly expressed in Cocteau's lengthiest critique of Freud in the first chapter of the *Journal d'un inconnu*, "De l'invisibilité," in which Freud is demoted from a scientist working "archaeologically" to a common looter of furniture. Cocteau here emphasizes that the night of which he speaks must not be confused with the night into which Freud calls upon his patients to descend. The night that occupies him is different: "La nuit dont je m'occupe est différente." No doctor here, no neurosis: "Non pas un docteur, ni une névrose."[33] In ironic allusion to the cathartic element of Freud's psychoanalysis, he calls this a "purgatory," tailored to the tastes of the masses ("à la mesure du grand nombre"). All Freud has done is furnish his contemporaries with "a confessional, easily accessible," in the method of free speech that seems to bring relief. This is the sum total of the gain Freud's work offers to his patients. For himself, the gain (Cocteau is here pursuing his "furniture" metaphor) lies in acquiring what he can of the "intérieur" of his patients and then exhibiting the results of his work in a furniture depot: "Freud's fault is to have made of our night a furniture warehouse which discredits it."[34] Freud, he says, has rummaged around in meager apartments and picked up a few furnishings of mediocre quality and some erotic photographs ("Freud cambriolait de pauvres appartements. Il en déménageait quelques meubles médiocres et des photographies érotiques"); but he did not welcome the great disorder he found. He never recognized the supersensible in anomaly, never sanctioned the abnormal as transcendental: "Il ne consacra jamais l'anormal en tant que transcendance. Il ne salua pas les grands désordres."[35] In contrast to Cocteau's own undertaking, Freud was only ever in search of the visible: "À l'encontre de notre étude, il ne recherche que la visibilité."[36]

Cocteau's repudiations of Freud have in no way hampered psychoanalytical readings of his own work. On the contrary, scholars have repeatedly interpreted his works by using analytical vocabulary and by putting the poet himself "on the couch"—not least to determine his position with regard to myth in his own life and works.[37] Readings of this kind come as no surprise. It stands to reason to wish to interpret Cocteau's oeuvre, his dazzling odyssey through styles and artistic disciplines, as a reflection of his life, which was lived in a complex flux of interpersonal relations (mostly with men, but also with women). In view of his many appeals to his own mother and the plethora of women and maternal figures in his work—figures who regularly prove acquiescent and submissive or lofty and masterful in their encounters with male figures—one might well ask not only about narcissistic structures, but also, and especially, about the presence of the Oedipus complex in the poet's work. Klaus Rave, for instance, explores this in great depth in his psychoanalytical study of Cocteau. The result suggests that Cocteau's entire work bears witness to an ambivalence that is a result of a regressive Oedipal instinctual drive and failed attempts at its repression.[38]

If we take Rave's conclusions seriously, Cocteau appears in Freud's sense as a "psychoneurotic" who has not "succeeded" in solving the task with which he is faced, someone who could not overcome the Oedipus complex. Thus, the following diagnosis is made: In rejecting Freud's call to analysis, Cocteau failed as a solver of riddles; and instead of living rationally, he lived "addicted to neurosis," ensnared as if in myth, "in ignorance of the desires that offend morality, the desires that nature has forced upon us," incapable of "detaching" his "sexual impulses" from his mother.[39]

In view of this finding, and in regard to Cocteau's anti-Freudian venting, we might well ask: who should be defending himself against whom? But this would be to miss the point, just as it would be wrong to evaluate the artistic work and aims of Cocteau by psychological means alone or to approach Freud's project with a purely poetological method. It would disregard the fact that these are quite different worlds and worldviews, whose heterogeneous languages and topologies cannot simply be translated into the other without loss. Although Freud and Cocteau, at least on a superficial reading, sometimes use similar vocabulary (for example, figures of archaeology, the realm of dream and the "subconscious"), it should be clear by now just how incommensurable were the contexts of perspective and intention within which they respectively worked. No attempt will be made here to fabricate a reconciliation—by inflicting either a rationalistic enlightenment on the one or an artistic revelation of irrationality on the other. It would be fruitless to decide who was right and who was wrong.

Instead, it will suffice to note the striking nature of the opposition of "art versus science" found in Cocteau. Freud himself was always open to poetry and gratefully acknowledged that he had often encountered problems and behaviors in literature that were of importance in his work. Conversely, Freud's own influence on the arts and on literature, especially his work on dream and instinct, indeed, Freud's significance for the whole of twentieth-century intellectual life, is so obvious that it would be superfluous to give examples. It is enough to cite one early instance of reception in Thomas Mann's lecture "Freud's Position in the History of Modern Thought" (1929), in which Mann gives the scientist an artist's thanks for his insights and evaluates psychoanalysis in the context of recent intellectual history.

None of this, though, robs Cocteau's work of its intrinsic right to a prestigious place in the plurality of cultural universes. Were we to accept Rave's analyses, it would mean discounting Cocteau's entire work, even though he quite deliberately rejected Freud's claim to be a solver of riddles. Intent not on demystification but on mystification,[40] Cocteau made it his life's work from the mid-1920s on to bring mystery to bear in all its enigmatic power, to darken what seemed to be clear. Many of the poems he wrote in pursuit of this task shatter the shell of normal language and create a network of words, compound sentences, and clauses free of syntactic rules, in which self-referencing connections of signifier and signified are intentionally interrupted, made to refer to a different level of "sense" beyond the ordinary by means of the blatant non-sense of the prima facie signified.

Cocteau's aim here was to lead the hermeneutic quest for meaning and symbolism *ad absurdum*. At the same time he withdrew both his poetry and his own self (the poet of a *poésie* irreducible to conventional aspirations of comprehension) from any classificatory approach. Thus, as *poète*, he did not see himself as guarantor of a transitivity that binds an "other"—whether of this world or another—to itself as an object and to which it thereby certifies access.[41] Rather—as is shown by his continual efforts in his work to dissolve ordering concepts such as space, time, and causality, subject and object—Cocteau saw himself as a poet who, on encountering traditional patterns of thought and reception, would exert a dishabituating effect and, rising above the throng in this function, disclose unfamiliar perspectives.

We may take the poem "Rien ne cesse" as an example of this. The first two strophes are as follows:

> Rien ne cesse rien n'est les morts ne sont pas morts
> Les vivants s'imaginent vivre
> Un acte continue où l'on ne peut le suivre
> Rien n'est dedans rien n'est dehors.

> Rien ne pèse tout pèse et notre marche lourde
> Est légère dans le sommeil.
> Aveugles sont nos yeux et nos oreilles sourdes
> Dans un monde au rêve pareil.[42]

> Nothing ends nothing is the dead are not dead
> The living imagine themselves to live
> An act continues that cannot be followed
> Nothing inside nothing outside.

> Nothing weighs all weighs and our heavy tread
> Is light in sleep,
> Blind are our eyes and deaf our ears
> In a world akin to dream.

This poem, from the anthology *Clair-obscur*, whose poetic signature is strikingly colored by Cocteauesque enigma, reads like a program poem. It evokes the "monde au rêve pareil" to which Cocteau always tried to open himself in his creative work: a dreamlike "zone" between the visible and invisible worlds, in which our habits and so our habitual forms of perception dissolve. It is that "zone where the living are not living, where the dead are not dead"[43] familiar to us from the Orpheus texts and films. Speaking with André Fraigneau, Cocteau described it as follows: "The zone is 'made of the memories of mortals and the ruins of their habits.' It relies on no dogma. It is a no-man's-land between life and death. The instant of coma, one might say."[44]

The lines of this poem in a sense "exhibit" this no-man's-land between life and death, where one is neither fully dead nor truly alive. They show the reader that the poet (like the *poète* represented by the poet Cégeste in *Orphée* and *Le testament d'Orphée*) has come in touch with something that ordinary perceptions distort, that something is opening up a "new" dimension in and through his *poésie*, a dimension in which the stabilizing, signifying effect of oppositions is abolished. Dream and reality, day and night, interior and exterior, life and death are not diametrical opposites, but exist in a dynamic relationship so that the reader sees the reliable, ordered, and comprehensible act of reading slip away: "Rien ne cesse rien n'est les morts ne sont pas morts."

Cocteau's work with myths should also be seen in light of this aspiration of dishabituation. As enigmatic "disorders," they are directed against ordered attributions of unambiguous meanings, and hence against semantic ossification. Mythical narratives and individual my-themes, for instance in *Orphée*, are not invoked for purposes of stabiliza-tion, nor therefore, as might be feared, from a perspective sharpened by the historical events of the twentieth century, for purposes of a regres-sive mythology. Rather, here too, in his own specific "work on myth," Cocteau was concerned with destabilization—by overcoming ossified forms by means of a montage of excised ancient and modern fragments into a kaleidoscopic abundance of interrelation, facilitating their insta-bility.[45] To this end, he constantly created "zones" in his work, to pro-vide a locale for what lies between oppositions: liminal regions inhab-ited by liminal figures, characterized by inconclusiveness and ambiguity.

"Where dream and reality merge": Mythic Personalities between Dream and Reality

In his quest to implement this destabilizing principle, the realm and environs of film and theater offered Cocteau much inspiration and

constructed by the super ego.

scope for his own creativity, with the opportunities they furnished for visual portrayal and impact and the sensation regularly stirred up by celebrities. The dazzling mythical quality of many of Cocteau's characters has many analogies in the world of the stars of stage and screen. For instance, the appearances of the princess played by Maria Casarès in the film *Orphée* remind us of divas like Greta Garbo and especially Marlene Dietrich, whose aura of indeterminacy, a disquieting ambiguity, unmistakably hinted beyond traditional gender roles and social conventions of femininity. Film stars were even then what they still are today: living myths of enormous attraction. Society takes hold of them for the purpose of certain messages. Their bodies are employed in everyday culture to serve, in the words of Roland Barthes, as "mythical signs"; narratives connected with them establish a compelling model for the audience and provide them with answers to questions on the meaning of life.[46] The movie industry and popular press of Cocteau's time, which had already discovered the pull of the star's personality and developed methods to make film actors into stars and market them successfully,[47] staged "the Dietrich," as Germans sometimes call her, in lavish and fantastical garb. Intentionally made enigmatic by a particular dramaturgy of lighting in film and on photographs—sometimes reproducing traditional stereotypes of femininity and sometimes undermining them in a gentleman's attire—she became, even during her lifetime, a figure often referred to in everyday language as a "cult figure," "(living) legend" or "modern myth."[48]

Cocteau himself contributed to some of the "living legends" and myths of the day. It comes as no surprise that one of them was the myth of "the Dietrich." In appearance disdainful of traditional gender allocations, she must have struck Cocteau as a welcome embodiment of the zonal states he strove to portray. In a 1954 paean of praise to Dietrich, for example, he gives a description of the diva that plays with the incriminatory ambivalence of theriomorphic apparitions of femininity to infiltrate the visual aesthetic of hybrid creatures: "Marlene Dietrich . . . , Your name begins with a caress and ends with the crack of a whip. You wear feathers and furs that seem part of your body like the fur of the wildcat and the feathers of a bird."[49] The "fur of the wildcat" evokes the predator, the "feathers of a bird" a feminine, avian apparition that is as inexact as the descriptions of many hybrid beings since antiquity, not least the Sphinx. Cocteau invokes her iconography here, while also leading the imaginations of his readers from the winged predator-woman to another domain of doom and destruction, the deadly seductions of the Lorelei's voice and gaze: "Votre voix, votre regard sont ceux de Lorelei." But he does this only to highlight the genuinely humane qualities of the human Dietrich, and to insist on aspects of her that, outside the "myth" created about and around her, show her as an individual living and working beyond collective myths and cultural imaginations of "fatal femininity": "But the Lorelei was dangerous. You are not; for the secret of your beauty lies in taking care of your heart line. It is your heart line [*ligne de cœur*] that places you above elegance, above fashions, above styles. Above, even, your courage, your gait, your films and your songs."[50]

With the "ligne de cœur," Cocteau draws a demarcating line between the rhetorical myths of fatal femininity and Marlene the actual human being. So this praise to the diva is not to be seen as a reactionary, mythifying act, but on the contrary, its purpose is to subject that principle to a destabilizing montage. As a first step, Cocteau plays on fantasy images belonging to the sphere of traditional collective myths of the "threatening," culminating in a comparison with the Lorelei founded on the *tertium comparationis* of voice and gaze. The second step then brings a clear distancing process, with the individual "Marlene Dietrich" distinguished from the collective myth "Lorelei." Thirdly and finally, the images Cocteau uses to compare with the diva—"poisson chinois," say, or "oiseau-lyre"—tend to evoke a spirit of poetic effervescence, rather than myths of the "femme fatale," citing a variety of the star's movie successes.

Cocteau was fully aware of the quasi-religious function of modern myths like that of Dietrich. He saw them as mythical "lies-truths" (*mensonges-vérités*) fabricated by the media, and he saw their creation as a sign of the age, characterized by a loss of religious values and spiritual direction. Another prominent star figure appears in his notes on actors and directors as an outstanding example of a personal *mensonge-vérité*, today one of the best known of all French "living legends": Brigitte Bardot. Cocteau wrote his short gloss on Bardot in 1962, after penning similar brief articles on other cult figures of the movie world, including Charlie Chaplin and James Dean.[51] His words stylize the actress, like Dietrich or the Princesse in *Orphée*, as a "zonal creature," as he seeks to place her at the limen between dream and reality, that is, at the place where our ordinary forms of perception dissolve:

> One of the signs of our times is to create immediate myths in all spheres. The press takes it upon itself to invent certain persons who exist and to deck them out with an imaginary life superimposed upon the one they live. Brigitte Bardot offers us a perfect example of this curious admixture. It is probable that destiny has placed her at the very place where dream and reality merge. Her beauty and her talent are indisputable, but she also has some other intangible thing that attracts the idolaters of an age deprived of gods.[52]

Cocteau's positioning of Brigitte Bardot "à la place exacte où le rêve et la réalité se confondent," in an "âge privé de dieux," incidentally corresponds to his own situation. The very place where Cocteau located Bardot as *mythe* was the same place where, according to his own view of himself, he himself was located. From there, he created and worked as the *poète* whose *mythe* he was continually inventing, as Arthur B. Evans has shown in the example of *Orphée*.[53] Cocteau's own myth is that of a quasi-Orphic "zonal creature" who, in an age deprived of its gods, has access to the world to which those gods have withdrawn—and to the "unknown" in general—and who responds to the urgent need to bring secrets to light and to tell them to all ("urgence de mettre des secrets au grand jour et de les confier à tous").[54] In accordance with Cocteau's sense of himself as a poet of mythical quality drawing on the reserves of the *moi obscur* in the modern world, his *poésie* "brings to light" ancient mythology and "modern myths" alike.[55] His poetry interweaves figures and elements of Greco-Roman provenance with modern cult figures and objects such as movie stars of the time and fetishized objects of the technological, industrialized world, for example, the Rolls-Royce—a typical mythical object in the Barthesian sense—with its radio as the talking conveyance of the Princesse in *Orphée*. Through merging the ancient and the modern, Cocteau hoped to create a timeless, "mythical" consciousness, in the sense of the dream aesthetic described above—a consciousness in which the boundaries of past and present, reality and fictionality, actuality and appearance, inner and outer world would be abolished.

As we have seen, Cocteau found theater and film to be particularly suitable for creating such a "mythical-actual" reality and presenting it directly to the eyes. And he made determined use of their technological possibilities in order to reveal what he regarded as the indistinguishability of reality and poetry "to the naked eye." In making films, the camera served as a vehicle ultimately capable of permitting everyone to dream the same dream together, "a dream that is not a dream of sleep but a waking dream," perhaps a dream that is "more true than the truth."[56] In stage productions, he used light and sound (record players and loudspeakers), sets, and symbolic props to conjure all manner of sensory illusions and hallucinations, thereby maneuvering performers and fixtures into constellations devised to portray transits of the threshold between the visible and invisible worlds.

"An Oedipus and the Sphinx*": Cocteau's* Machine infernale

The theme of transits between the visible and invisible, inner and outer worlds, between actuality and appearance, also runs as a leitmotif through the four acts of *La machine infernale*. This theatrical piece, completed in 1932 and first performed in 1934 at the Louis Jouvet Theater in Paris, is a very free—indeed farcical—adaptation of the ancient Oedipus material, in which the mythical Oedipus-Sphinx configuration is of central importance. Cocteau had long intended to stage this configuration from his own, new perspective. Back in 1928, he had already intimated that he dreamed of writing "an *Œdipe et le Sphinx*, a sort of tragi-comic prologue to *Oedipus the King*."[57] It is this tragicomedy that comprises the first three acts of *La machine infernale*. The fourth act is a "contraction" of Sophocles' tragedy fully in line with Cocteau's "esthétique du minimum,"[58] similar to the play begun in 1921–1922 *Œdipe Roi*, with the subtitle *Adaption libre d'après Sophocle*.

The first act of *La machine infernale* already presents the play's central theme of transits between the visible and invisible, inner and outer worlds. It focuses on a harbinger spirit, the ghost of Laïus, who is probably seen by some *dramatis personae* but not by others, and certainly not by the one to whom his warning applies: Jocaste. The apparition of the ghost derives from Seneca.[59] In his *Oedipus*, the conjuration of the ghost of Laius is intended to clarify the identity of the regicide, a motif also taken up by Corneille and Voltaire.[60] In Cocteau's version, one thing above all becomes clear with the ghost—which here appears of its own accord: the inability to see or hear him is due to a particular incapacity that Jocaste shares with the protagonist Œdipe, the incapacity to perceive the world beyond the visible. Both Jocaste and Œdipe lack the ability of introspection. They also lack any openness to transcendental knowledge and are therefore hesitant to accept mental or physical change. The aging Jocaste who wants to stay young forever loves strapping muscles. In erotic desire and longing for her long-lost son, she keeps grabbing soldiers of his age by the thighs—incest already rearing its head. The boastful Œdipe cockily maintains a faked Hercules image that he has created for himself, and he wants to play King with the Queen without taking any responsibility. Thus embroiled in vanities, fears, and superficialities, Jocaste and Œdipe each construct their own personal hell, their "infernum," contributing to the realization of the "infernal" plan of the "fate machine," "one of the most perfect machines ever devised by the infernal gods for the mathematical annihilation of a mortal." This, at least, is how the tragic events are glossed in a prophetic summary by the offstage voice, "La voix," which addresses the audience. Spoken by Cocteau himself in 1934, "La voix" functions as an epic theatrical element in the play, focusing the action wholly on the clockwork regularity of the mechanism of the "infernal machine": "Regarde, spectateur, [...] une de plus parfaites machines construites par les dieux infernaux pour l'anéantissement mathématique d'un mortel."[61]

A structural comparison of Cocteau's play and Sophocles' model makes clear the intended meaning of "La voix" to the audience at the beginning of the play. The process of the "infernal machine" is marked by the same tragic finality as the action of *Oedipus the King*. Events approach the catastrophic telos with relentless linearity. The action proceeds as it does in order to fulfill the laws of tragedy with technical precision. Œdipe and Jocaste here stand as symbols of people carried away into their calamity—hurtling, blinded, on toward their tragic fall.

To this extent, Cocteau's portrayal is similar to that of Sophocles.

Yet, it differs significantly in the tragicomedy and "dis-enchantment" of the characters systematically deployed from the first through third and even final acts. All figures, including Œdipe, are caricatured to a grotesque extreme, degraded to bizarre marionettes of an infernal nexus of delusion.[62] The protagonist is not presented as a great hero falling victim to an extraordinary fate, but as a petty and self-centered figure bent on power and glory. Seen in this way, Œdipe resembles Seneca's Oedipus, but lacks any of the dimensions of a king. Accordingly, he is also innocent of the despotic traits of Seneca's Oedipus. Cocteau's Œdipe is no forbidding despot, but a little squirt. His hubris does not consist, like that of Sophocles' Oedipus, in overestimating his own de facto intelligence. Œdipe has no such intelligence, but thrives through particularly ridiculous misapprehensions of situations, and misinterpretations of his actions. Like his mother, he undergoes only superficial change, while living in inner stagnation. The hubris of both Jocaste and Œdipe lies in their failure to deal with their issues (in Jocaste's case, aging and death; for Œdipe, assuming responsibility as a person and a man). To compensate for their deficits, they instead seek refuge in each other (Jocaste's indulgence in youth, Œdipe's in the maternal embrace). They ignore all the hints and reminders offered to them from the supernatural side as events progress, and thereby evade all insight and opportunity for real change. In act 1 ("Le fantôme"), the ghost of the murdered Laïus appears—in vain—to warn of the impending disaster. His message to Jocaste goes unheard. In act 3 ("La nuit des noces"), the wedding night of Œdipe and Jocaste, following the intoxication of the festivities the bride and groom sink down in leaden fatigue as a storm sweeps by, bringing menacing peals of thunder. Fearful dreams assail them, in which further signs attest to what they fail to perceive while awake. But these nocturnal omens and signals to recognition remain unacknowledged, just as the warnings of the blind seer Tirésias are dismissed as the ramblings of an old fool and the drunkard's songs of mothers and sons at the end of the party go unnoticed. Only seventeen years later do insight and recognition dawn. In act 4 ("Œdipe Roi"), Œdipe at first joyfully welcomes the news of the death of his supposed father, as he now thinks the oracle's prophecy that he would murder his father and marry his mother cannot possibly come true. But the celebrations merely pave the way for the impending twist. A messenger announces the truth. Jocaste hangs herself. Œdipe blinds himself.

The finale that follows the catastrophe once more brings the focus sharply on the subject of transits between the visible and invisible, inner and outer worlds. It presents a transfigured Œdipe and the ghost of a transfigured Jocaste. Now having accepted the true course of things, they open themselves to the spheres of alternative knowledge beyond the visible world and find themselves consciously between life and death, "where dream and reality melt into one." As Jocaste's spirit and Œdipe's daughter Antigone lead the blinded Œdipe into the city[63]—leading to the poets, to the pure hearts ("aux poètes, aux cœurs purs") with whom they are now kin, according to Tirésias—Œdipe can see the ghost of his mother.[64] The scene demonstrates how a man became human by accepting his fate. This, Jocaste explains, is because he is now blind-seeing, like Tirésias: "You see me because you are blind; the others cannot see me any longer." The ensuing dialogue of son and mother concludes with a comment by Créon, brother of Jocaste, recalling act 1 and the "Fantôme" of Laïus: "He [Œdipe] is speaking with ghosts, he is delirious, he has a fever."[65] Créon here, untransfigured and far removed from the acceptance of the course of events to which Jocaste and Œdipe have come, represents the purely materialistic worldview previously held by the two now transfigured. At the end of the play, then, in anticipation of a new mathematical cycle of the infernal fate machine, this time on the blinded Créon, we see again an indication of the disaster that results from the inability to open oneself to the invisible world.

The dismantling of the Oedipus figure is strikingly apparent in act 2 ("La rencontre d'Œdipe et du Sphinx"). In terms of the play's genesis, the Oedipus-Sphinx constellation staged here is the starting point of the drama; in terms of structure and content, it is its crossroads, pivot, and lynchpin. This was Cocteau's primary preoccupation when he decided to write an *Œdipe et le Sphinx*. This above all was to be the content of the play whose performance Cocteau envisaged, as early as 1928, as moving between the surface of farce and the depths of tragedy: "allant de la farce au comble de la tragédie."[66] In the final version too, *La machine infernale*, the mythical constellation has a key function as the fate machinery grinds on, relentlessly crushing the man: the portrayal of

Œdipe before the Sphinx brings the association between clumsiness and a purpose-oriented rationalism into particularly clear focus—an association that is central to the tragedy of Œdipe. Œdipe appears in all his weakness and vanity. His blind determination before the Sphinx to win renown and power proves to be a driving force in the wheel-work of the *machine infernale*, which runs like clockwork until it destroys him.

Deprived of Categorization by Basic Principles: *"Œdipe et le Sphinx"* on the Threshold

The encounter between Œdipe and the Sphinx also has a prominent position in the structure of the drama and the topography of dramatic action Cocteau designed. The meeting takes place between the first act, in which Œdipe's murdered father Laïus appears as a ghost, and the third, Œdipe's wedding night with his mother. Structurally speaking, the encounter forms the keystone in the arch of the three scenes that precede the catastrophe. This position makes its function as a dramatic threshold leading from the patricide to the maternal incest directly apparent. The liminal character of the encounter is also emphasized by the multilayered mythotopography of the "between," which, already present in antiquity, becomes sharply profiled in the play, both spatially and figuratively, and is now brought to striking fruition. The scene before the "portes de Thèbes" unfolds, according to the stage directions, in a lonely place on a hill overlooking the city, at dead of night by moonlight: "Décor: un lieu désert, sur une éminence qui domine Thèbes, au clair de lune."[67] There, "in the forbidden zone,"[68] Œdipe's "encounter" with the Sphinx takes place amid ruins, the remains of a small temple with wrecked columns and a collapsed wall ("décombres d'un petit temple, un mur en ruine"), in other words in a similar liminal region to the "zone" in *Orphée*, "made of humans' memory and the ruin of their customs."[69] The "zonal" signature of both the periphery of Thebes in *La machine infernale* and the no-man's-land behind the mirror in *Orphée*, is characterized by twilight and ruins: by the twilight that signals the transition from light to dark, day to night, life to death (and in each case vice versa), and by the ruins as signifiers of a "between" linking the persistence of form and collapse (*ruine*), memory and present, destruction and new beginning, mourning and the longing for redemption.[70]

Another detail helps to sharpen the topographical contours of the "between" by comparison with ancient accounts. This is the presence in the venue outside Thebes (which lighting and set define as a transitional zone) of another liminal figure alongside the Sphinx: Anubis. The interplay of the two intensifies the "sphinginity" of the Sphinx. Their interaction intercuts the mythology of Greece with that of Egypt. Moreover, the physiognomy of the jackal-headed Anubis is monstrous. It is not possible definitively to determine whether he is deity, human, or animal. These definitions are fluid, since, as a deity, he—like the Sphinx he here accompanies—can take on anthropomorphic or theriomorphic forms. The "chimaeric," aggregate apparition of the two hints at the coexistence of a visible this-worldly side and a spiritual sphere in the beyond that is invisible (to most people). The fact that Anubis and the Sphinx pass between these two spheres and in doing so can appear either in earthly human/animal form or unearthly divine form (despite all the human traits of the Sphinx) points to their superior level of being, which becomes increasingly clear throughout the play and is fully revealed at the end. In this way, the play stages and discloses mankind's participation in the monstrous.

Anubis is an Egyptian deity who was portrayed in antiquity mostly as a prone black dog or jackal, or as a man with a dog's or jackal's head (Lucian uses the word κυνοπρόσωπος, "dog-faced").[71] As a figure of death, protector of necropoleis, and judge and guardian of the dead, he represents the gateway to the beyond. The oldest epithets associated with him, such as "lord of the land apart" and "who is upon his mountain," also locate him as an inhabitant of the mountains of the desert.[72] To some extent, these attributes, all indications of a liminal figure, align him mythologically with the Sphinx, and this may have led Cocteau to assign him to her—the ῥαψῳδός κύων (Sophocles), the "bitch who sings, as they say"—"chienne qui chante, comme ils disent" (Cocteau).[73] By the side of the "singing bitch," the "dog-faced one" watches over the events at Thebes, over life and death—and even over the person and office of the Sphinx herself. At the beginning of act 2, shortly before Œdipe's appearance as the first of three signals sounds announcing the impending closure of the gates of Thebes, it is also this function that makes Anubis remind the Sphinx that she must fulfill her duties until the gates are completely shut: "Il en reste encore deux [sonneries] avant la fermeture des portes de Thèbes."[74] Later, too, he shows himself to be a watchman of discipline, attention, clarity of perception, and insight. He acts as a kind of gatekeeper, insisting on absolute respect—even from the Sphinx herself—for the threshold on which he stands and to whose existence his rule is essential. He constantly nurtures composure, exhibiting tactical superiority and transcendental abilities. For instance, he surveys the story of Œdipe's life from his birth, exposure, and adoption, through the incest, the birth of children, and the suicide of Jocaste, to his death: "De sa naissance à sa mort la vie d'Œdipe s'étale, sous mes yeux."[75] In the Anubis-Sphinx "working partnership," his is the directly terrifying role: the mythical power of death, as it were, biting with a jackal's jaws, ripping into and dismembering the whole body of the individual.

The Sphinx herself is, in Cocteau's play, another manifestation of the Greek goddess of vengeance, Nemesis. As daughter of Night (Nyx) and sister of Sleep (Hypnos) and Death (Thanatos),[76] she too can easily be seen to have a liminal function, like Anubis and her ancient predecessor, the Greco-Theban Sphinx. According to the ancient view as conveyed by literature, her task—as Nemesis—is above all to punish humans for arrogance, hubris, and defiance of Themis, the Greek goddess of law and custom, and in general to avenge wrongful conduct toward the gods and other mortals.[77] Equipped with pelt and feathers, according to Cocteau's stage directions, as theriomorphic attributes of the Sphinx, this Nemesis-Sphinx appears alternately as a goddess and a white-clad seventeen-year-old girl. Cocteau himself indicated her close kinship to the Princesse in *Orphée*: "Le Sphinx agit comme agira la princesse dans mon film *Orphée*."[78] Like the Princesse, he understands her too to be a mediator between mortals and gods, and ultimately subject to a higher authority. It must be added that she too (like the Princesse in *Orphée*) is allowed a helper in her work (of bringing death), a helper who (like the "angel of death" Heurtebise in *Orphée*) is reminiscent of Hermes. The Greeks equated Anubis with Hermes Psychopompos, who led the souls of the dead into or back out of the underworld.[79] Like the Princesse, "Madame La Mort," Nemesis-Sphinx works in close contact with her helper and keeps nothing secret from him. Tired of her role as murderous purveyor of riddles, she questions her own rule and that of Anubis, as well as his appearance: "Anubis, pourquoi ta tête de chien? Pourquoi le dieu des morts sous l'apparence que lui supposent les hommes crédules? Pourquoi en Grèce un dieu d'Egypte?"[80] Anubis' attempt to make her see "raison" is fruitless. The Sphinx longs for requited love with a mortal. Insofar as she is Nemesis, she wishes for death, because she no longer wants to kill. Insofar as she is a girl, she wants to live on and love in her mortal form. The arrival of Œdipe is thus timely. In him, she hopes to find this fulfillment of her longing. She loves as the death of Orphée—the Princesse—loves Orphée. But ultimately, she sacrifices the mortal figure. She abandons the interim state between mortals and gods to endure as goddess.

Besides these spatial and character-related aspects that highlight the liminal nature of the encounter scene, there are also threshold elements related to action—that is, elements that slow down the action. During the encounter, there are three instances of a situation where events could take a turn that would defeat the fulfillment of the oracle. Œdipe receives three "chances" and squanders them all. So the transit of the "threshold to disaster" in each case is postponed, adding emphasis to the liminal situation.

Events leading up to the first "chance" proceed as follows. The Sphinx is busy complaining of her suffering to Anubis as Œdipe arrives. He does not recognize her, because she is currently in her guise as girl, and he confidently tells her of his intention to defeat the Sphinx in order to win the hand of Jocaste. "The conqueror of the Sphinx, would he be the first one you see? I know the reward. The queen is promised to him" (*Machine infernale*, 76). At this point, the Sphinx makes a first serious attempt to prevent Œdipe from crossing the threshold into incestuous calamity, by making a play for him as a woman. When Œdipe declares that he will marry Jocaste, she objects, "A woman who could be your mother!" (75). But he replies simply, "What is essential is that she may not be" (76). Undeterred, she suggests to Œdipe that he should not pursue his quest for renown, but should foil the oracle ("déjouer l'oracle") and marry a younger woman. But Œdipe rejects her: "Voici une parole qui ne vous ressemble pas. La parole d'une mère de Thèbes" (77). He sticks to his intention of following the task he has set himself and marrying Jocaste. The first chance to avert the prophecy is gone.

The second chance comes before the riddle is uttered. Rejected by Œdipe, the Sphinx does not hesitate to take her form as Nemesis to intimidate him and to effect a situation in which he, incapable of solving her riddle, will be condemned to death. But because she loves him, she means to release him as "free" (84f.)—after making him whimper for mercy—without subjecting him to the test. At this point, Anubis intervenes. "Pardon me, Sphinx. This man cannot leave from here without undergoing a trial" (85). The Sphinx, who has previously revealed to Œdipe the solution to the riddle during a trial run, now tells him the riddle, which he solves. Without the intervention of Anubis, Œdipe would have emerged from the encounter without having solved the riddle. He could therefore have claimed no victory, and made no claim for the prize on offer—the hand of Jocaste.

Œdipe squanders the third chance even without the help of Anubis. After running back to his helper, immediately after solving the riddle, without so much as glancing back, he now turns around—and only now comes the death of the Sphinx in her shape as girl. Here too, Cocteau inventively adapts the mythical tradition. After another rush of hope, as lover, when Œdipe turns, and ready to give him another chance, the Sphinx must accept that he turned not out of attraction or gratitude to her, but in order to claim her dead body as proof of his supposed "victory"—she must recognize, in other words, that Œdipe is beyond saving in his brazenness. The Sphinx now gives up her girl guise, and with this sacrifice of her mortal body fully becomes the goddess of vengeance that she is. She gives her corpse the mortal head of Anubis, on the grounds that the mob would stone Œdipe to death if he came to Thebes carrying the body of a young girl instead of the monster the people expect ("en place du monstre auquel les hommes s'attendent") (91). Œdipe does not see through these events. He fails to recognize the Sphinx as the goddess of vengeance who will henceforth accompany him. In vain self-delusion, he takes the dead body of the girl and hurries eagerly to Thebes with his "trophy" to boast of his "victory"—hastening into the catastrophe, when his ascent to victory will be revealed as a descent to destruction. Until this revelation he will remain blind, *aveugle*, as the Sphinx concludes: one of those mortals who, as Anubis puts it, are born blind and never notice, until one day the truth bursts open their eyes: "Many men are born blind, and they may perceive this only on the day when truth puts out their eyes" (92).

The dismantling of the Oedipus figure could hardly be clearer. Cocteau reduces the ancient hero by caricature to a braggart vainly intent on achieving renown, who before the Sphinx cuts the most lamentable figure imaginable. For instance, when the Sphinx shifts shape from girl to goddess (in the moment I have characterized as the "second chance") and rises up on illuminated wings, shrieking with a terrifying voice, Œdipe bursts into tears and cries for his mother. Yet no sooner has the Sphinx's utterance of the riddle brought him back to his senses than he has the effrontery to declaim the solution that the Sphinx has already given him, slap himself proudly on the chest and cry "Vainqueur!" (85). And finally, when the body of the Sphinx-girl has collapsed, dead, he lifts it, as Hercules lifted the body of the Nemean Lion, onto his shoulder. Thus, he thinks, he will look like a demigod and can enter Thebes in a manner befitting the situation. He marches away with prideful words—"I've killed the filthy beast!" "I've saved the city!" "I shall marry Queen Jocaste!" and "I will be king!"—statements ironized by Anubis's laconic aside, "Il est for-mi-da-ble" (93). Œdipe is for all the world like a colonial hunter who has defeated the Beast and enslaved the Other. Recalling how traditional images of masculinity and femininity were being mobilized for legitimizing purposes in all kinds of contexts in Cocteau's day, not least political, we can see how, in this final image of the act, Cocteau also delivers a resounding blow to colonialism, in which old gender patterns of masculinity as "culture" and femininity as "nature" were played out.

The Sphinx emerges from Cocteau's depiction of the mythical constellation in much better shape than Œdipe. Apart from the ghost of Laïus, whose warnings to his wife go unheard, the Sphinx is probably the only figure in the play who invites sympathy. It is significant in this regard that, like Laïus, who moves as a ghost between life and death, she too is a figure of the "between" that is, as someone who cares. Even in her guise as goddess of vengeance she has compassion for mortals. Her last words before leaving the earth with the god Anubis are "Poor, poor, poor men. . . . I can't go on, Anubis. . . . I'm suffocating. Let's leave this earth!" (93). Like the ghost of Laïus, she too remains opaque to understanding her hybrid existence. This hybridity manifests itself on several levels. More than just divine, human and animal traits merge within her. In yet another expression of Cocteau's predilection for interim and liminal states, which he articulates in so many ways, her gender too cannot be absolutely determined. Grammatically speaking, the French word "sphinx" is masculine, and the Sphinx herself says, at the end of act 2, that *the* (masculine) vanquished one is a woman: "Le vaincu est une femme" (90). Here too, then, there is a transit of a threshold between two "spheres," the masculine and the feminine. Ultimately, *the* (masculine) feminine Sphinx is vanquished and not vanquished, dead and immortal—in brief, a being existing in a "zone, où les vivants ne sont pas vivants, où les morts ne sont pas morts"[81]—and, as such a zonal being, excepted from categorization according to basic principles that are defined by that which they exclude.

Cocteau's Sphinx, then, is not as might be expected a conservative reformulation of an imago of mythified femininity. "Le Sphinx" does appear, in her encounter with Œdipe, as a representation of natural/demonic femininity typical of the conventional myths of the feminine that were circulating in literature and art in the first quarter of the twentieth century. But even here, as with Marlene Dietrich, Cocteau's business is not to give his seal of approval to the products of thousands of years of male perspectives on woman in art and literature.[82] Rather, his overt elaboration of preconceived ideas contributes to a dissolution of the conventional semantics of those ideas, because it lifts the veil on the projective mechanisms of such mythifications of femininity. Thus, we see staged in this encounter of "Œdipe et le Sphinx" the process by which tensions arising from a gender conflict transmute into mythical images that are culturally dictated. We see how the Sphinx, who first appears to Œdipe as girl and woman, and then manifests herself with feathers and pelt as goddess of vengeance, exploits the cultural repertoire of images in order to appear threatening. She makes herself visible before Œdipe's mind's eye as a demonic figure in which all conceivable projections of threat converge:

> more nimble than a blind man, swifter than a gladiator's net, subtler than lightning, stiffer than a coachman, heavier than a cow, more dili-

gent than a schoolboy who pokes his tongue out as he does his sums, more draped with rigging and sails, more anchored, more rocking than a ship, more incorruptible than a judge, more voracious than insects, more bloodthirsty than birds, more nocturnal than an egg, more ingenious than Chinese executioners, more treacherous than the heart, more nonchalant than a trickster's hand, more fateful than the stars, more attentive than the snake moistening its prey with saliva. I secrete, I spin, I pay out, I wind, I unwind, I rewind, so that it is enough for me to want these knots for them to come about and to think of them for them to tighten or loosen; so fine that it escapes you, so soft that you imagine yourself a victim of a poison [. . .] conjured like the settings of our dreams, and above all invisible, invisible and majestic.[83]

With Œdipe still not petrified by fear following this hypnotic barrage of images, the Sphinx goes on, intensifying her threat even further to evoke in images practices traditionally ascribed to women and goddesses since antiquity, images associated with feminine guile, the power of seduction, and enigmatic and involute prophecy:

And I talk, I work, I wind, I unwind, I calculate, I meditate, I braid, I tease, I knit, I plait, I cross, I recross, I tie and untie and retie, [. . .] I entangle, I disentangle, I unlace, lace up, and start again; and I adjust, I cluster, I bind, I strap, I shackle, I accumulate, until you feel, from the tips of your toes to the roots of your hair, that you are wrapped in all the coils of one single reptile whose slightest breath chokes yours.[84]

The success of this second salvo is tremendous. Whereas before, Œdipe was still protesting and writhing in anger, he now whispers weakly, "Let me go! Mercy . . . !"—and then, "Mérope! . . . Maman!"[85] Cocteau makes clear here how images connoted as feminine in the mind of a masculine subject are capable, once his position or identity is insecure, of unleashing their power. He uses the example of Œdipe before the Sphinx to show the audience that the more insecure a position or identity is, the stronger is the assault of images of demonized threat and the stronger too is the need for integrative ideal images like that of the mother. With the visible enforcement of this idea, Cocteau lifts the veil on the projective mechanisms of attachment to images of mythified femininity. He thereby initiates a process of destabilization in those mechanisms. Once again, the audience is urged to examine collective myths and "hypnoses" with a critical mind—as Cocteau unambiguously put it later, in 1949, with the memories of World War II still fresh in the mind: "I earnestly desire that the French public should be insusceptible to collective hypnosis, should resist it with all the powers of their individualism and prove its intelligence by its criticism."[86]

Coda II: With Sophocles contra Freud: Cocteau's Work of Enlightenment

Like Freud, Cocteau was also doing the "work of enlightenment" in his own way, but his manner did not make use of rational and analytical methods. Instead, with art his method opened us to a new world, using poetic imagination and dismantling received attitudes through satire. Cocteau enlightens us by showing us the "infernal machine" we carry within ourselves, a mechanism that we have made ourselves in our intrigues, vanities, fears, and—this key message runs like a thread through Cocteau's work—in our lack of aptitude for supramental perception. He shows us that feted heroes are not necessarily heroes, that conquerors of the Sphinx are not necessarily triumphant, that there is something to discover beyond the sphere accessible to everyday reason, as we recognize the inextricability of poetry and reality—something inconsistent with conventional pretensions and attributes.

It must have been particularly appealing for Cocteau to bring Oedipus and the Sphinx together in a constellation that exposes all their indeterminacy and ambiguity. Both figures demonstrate liminality with particular clarity, and both are especially apt for creating, whether on the stage or in the mind of the recipient, a zone or no-man's-land that offers a venue akin to dream for that which lies between oppositions. It is likely that Cocteau welcomed the shock to the ordered world of living beings offered by the composite appearances of the Sphinx and Anubis. That Œdipe, in the presence of both, only superficially achieves a transition, failing to do so *inwardly*, that his victory over the Sphinx is no victory at all, that he achieves no development in his relationship with Jocaste but, as Freud would put it, remains trapped in the Oedipal problem of infancy. In short, that he *internally* stays caught in a liminal existence outside the boundaries of society, makes Cocteau's play (to us, today) much more directly intelligible than Sophocles' *Oedipus the King*.

In a sense, Cocteau in his *Machine infernale* turned "avec Sophocle contre Freud." With the arrangement of machine-like linearity and finality as destiny ultimately fulfilled, his construction coincides with that of Sophocles, even if in its modernity it unmistakably deviates from the Greek tragedian's ideas in various respects. Cocteau's tendency to deploy Sophocles against Freud is also evident in his *Journal d'un inconnu*. Here he claims that Freud, with his theory of the Oedipus complex, would almost accord with his (Cocteau's) approach, mindful of the spirit of the ancient tragedians, except for the fact that Sophocles believed in external destiny: "En ce qui concerne le complexe d'Œdipe, Freud coïnciderait presque avec notre ligne [. . .], si Sophocle n'avait pas cru au destin extérieur." Cocteau argues that his own drama has intensified still further the cruelly farcical element in the myth dramatized by the ancient tragedian, by portraying the hero's victory over the Sphinx as a phantom victory born of Œdipe's pride: "J'ai compliqué l'atroce farce dans *la Machine Infernale*, en faisant de la victoire d'Œdipe sur le Sphinx, une victoire postiche née de son orgueil."[87]

This treatment of the Oedipus figure clearly betrays Cocteau's view of himself as a dishabituating poet, the essence of whose poetic work was to use myths (or their repositioned fragments) to counter ingrained ways of seeing and thinking, and hence also to counter the appropriation of myth, in particular its annexation by the conservative culture of the French elites, as well as the "hermeneutic claim to absolute validity" of psychoanalysis and its remythifying tendencies. So Cocteau, in *La machine infernale*, decisively debunks the ancient Oedipus and the modern solver of riddles and conqueror of the Sphinx that Freud felt himself to be. Through the ridicule of caricature, he calls into question the conventional gender images and roles that Freud was still citing ancient myth to confirm. Cocteau's Œdipe is certainly not the solver of riddles who is "first in power" above all men (ὃς τὰ κλείν' αἰνίγματ' ᾔδει καὶ κράτιστος ἦν ἀνήρ)—the Sophoclean hero with whom Freud identified and whom he believed to have surpassed. Œdipe does not remotely understand who he is. He has no clue who or what the Sphinx is, nor does he care. By the same token, Cocteau's Sphinx can certainly not be described as a woman who, a riddle in her own right, is unable to solve herself and must solicit the help of male solvers of riddles. Rather, "Le Sphinx"—this ultimately triumphant bearer of theriomorphic attributes indicating divinity and hence knowledge and abilities reserved for immortals alone— has the knowledge Œdipe lacks but needs, and she wants to give it to him. Opportunistically, Œdipe takes what he needs of it to serve his purpose of attaining renown and power—but he learns nothing. He solves the riddle not with his own analytical faculties, but by having the answer at the ready at the right moment, an answer revealed to him by his female helper—"Le Sphinx" herself, Nemesis in girl form. As his aside shows ("That's too stupid!"), when the answer is given to him ("This animal is man"), he has understood nothing of what the solution means. Secure in his vain misapprehension of himself as solver of riddles and conqueror of the Sphinx, devoid of insight into his own existence and that of Nemesis-Sphinx, he leaves to show off his "achievements" and wallow in congratulations. Meanwhile, a gust of wind catches the two great gods, lifts them up—and day dawns.

Introduction

1. Milorad, "La clé des mythes dans l'oeuvre de Cocteau," *Cahiers Jean Cocteau* 2 (1971), 97–140, esp. 97.

2. See J. Boorsch, "The Use of Myths in Cocteau's Theatre," *Yale French Studies* 5 (1950), 75–81; L. Crowson, "The Role of Myth," in Crowson, *The Esthetic of Jean Cocteau* (Hanover, 1978), 124–161; B. Valette, "Modernité du mythe chez Cocteau," *Revue de l'Université de Bruxelles* 1–2 (1989), 7–22; H. Dumarty, "Le mythe dans l'oeuvre de Cocteau: La rencontre d'un signe et d'une intention," *Revue de l'Université de Bruxelles* 1–2 (1989), 23–40; G. Febel, "Mythen-Bricolage in Film und Theater Frankreichs—das Beispiel Jean Cocteau," in *Mythenkorrekturen: Zu einer paradoxalen Form der Mythenrezeption*, ed. M. Vöhler and B. Seidensticker (Berlin, 2005), 331–343.

3. For an overview of Oedipus' reception history, see N. Roßbach, *Mythos Ödipus: Texte von Homer bis Pasolini* (Leipzig, 2005); H. Hühn, "Oidipus," in *Mythenrezeption—Die antike Mythologie in Literatur, Kunst und Musik von den Anfängen bis zur Gegenwart* (*DNP*, Suppl. 5), ed. M. Moog-Grünewald (Stuttgart, 2008), 888–911. An overview of the Sphinx's reception history can be found in H. Demisch, *Die Sphinx: Geschichte ihrer Darstellung von den Anfängen bis zur Gegenwart* (Stuttgart, 1977); L. Winkler-Horaček, ed., *Wege der Sphinx: Monster zwischen Orient und Okzident* (Rahden, Westphalia, 2011).

4. Aristotle, *Poetics* 1452b–1453b, esp. 1453a10f. See H. Flashar, "König Ödipus: Drama und Theorie," *Gymnasium* 84 (1977), 120–136 (reprinted in *Eidola: Ausgewählte Kleine Schriften* [Amsterdam, 1989], 57–73); see also Flashar, "Die Poetik des Aristoteles und die griechische Tragödie," *Poetica* 16 (1984), 1–23.

5. For a brief overview, see N. Zink, *Sophokles: König Ödipus* (Frankfurt am Main, 1979), 79. There is a more extensive study by H. Hühn, in the article "Oidipus," mentioned in note 3. Studies on the literary reception of *Oedipus the King* are vast. The following is but a helpful selection: K. Hamburger, *Von Sophokles zu Sartre* (Stuttgart, 1962), 175–188; M. J. O'Brien, ed., *Twentieth Century Interpretations of Oedipus Rex: A Collection of Critical Essays* (Englewood Cliffs, NJ, 1968); C. Astier, *Le mythe d'Oedipe* (Paris, 1974); W. Theile, "Stoffgeschichte und Poetik: Literarischer Vergleich von Ödipusdramen (Sophokles, Corneille, Gide)," *arcadia* 10 (1975), 34– 51; M. Mueller, *Children of Oedipus and Other Essays on the Imitation of Greek Tragedy, 1550–1800* (Toronto, 1980), 105–152; L. Edmunds, *Oedipus: The Ancient Legend and Its Later Analogues* (Baltimore, 1985); J. Scherer, *Dramaturgies d'Oedipe* (Paris, 1987); C. Segal, *Oedipus Tyrannus: Tragic Heroism and the Limits of Knowledge* (New York, 1992), esp. 16–35 ("Reception and Influence") and 57–69 ("The Oedipus Myth and Its Interpretation"); D. Moddelmog, *Readers and Mythic Signs: The Oedipus Myth in Twentieth-Century Fiction* (Carbondale, 1993); G. Paduano, *Lunga storia di Edipo Re: Freud, Sofocle e il teatro occidentale* (Turin, 1994); R. D. Dawe, ed., *Sophocles: The Classical Heritage* (New York, 1996); T. Halter, *König Oedipus: Von Sophokles zu Cocteau* (Stuttgart, 1998); T. A. Szlezák, "Ödipus nach Sophokles," in *Antike Mythen in der europäischen Tradition*, ed. H. Hofmann (Tübingen, 1999), 199–220; A. Daskarolis, *Die Wiedergeburt des Sophokles aus dem Geist des Humanismus: Studien zur Sophokles-Rezeption in Deutschland vom Beginn des 16. bis Mitte des 17. Jahrhunderts* (Tübingen, 2000); E. Wesolowska, "The Image of Oedipus in Modern Literature," *Aufidus* 40 (2000), 79–88; M. Lurje, *Die Suche nach der Schuld: Sophokles' Oedipus Rex, Aristoteles' Poetik und das Tragödienverständnis der Neuzeit* (Munich, 2004); M. McDonald and M. Walton, eds., "The Dramatic Legacy of Myth: Oedipus in Opera, Radio, Television and Film," in *The Cambridge Companion to Greek and Roman Theatre* (Cambridge, 2007), 303–326.

6. On Cocteau's term "contraction," see D. Möller, *Jean Cocteau und Igor Strawinsky: Untersuchungen zur Ästhetik und zu "Oedipus Rex"* (Hamburg, 1981), 300f. The concept "contraction" comes from Cocteau himself; the principle of reworking corresponds to "concisions" in Gérard Genette's nomenclature of intertextual procedures. See W. Frick, *'Die mythische Methode': Komparatistische Studien zur Transformation der griechischen Tragödie im Drama der klassischen Moderne* (Tübingen, 1998), 336–344; G. Genette, *Palimpsestes: La littérature au second degré* (Paris, 1982), 271.

7. See D. Möller, *Jean Cocteau und Igor Strawinsky*, 300–314 (on *Antigone*), 314– 329 (on *Œdipe-Roi*), 331ff. (on *Oedipus Rex*). Further recommendations on *Œdipe-Roi* would be: T. W. Andrus, "Oedipus Revisited: Cocteau's 'Poésie de théâtre,'" *French Review* 48 (1975), 722–728; on Stravinsky's opera-oratorio: P. Bauschatz, "Œdipus: Stravinsky and Cocteau Recompose Sophocles," *Comparative Literature* 43 (1991), 150–170; K. Töchterle, "Wortgeklingel: Konstrukt oder Sprachmagie? Zum Libretto von Strawinskys *Oedipus Rex*," in *Resonanzen: Innsbrucker Beiträge zum modernen Musiktheater bei den Salzburger Festspielen*, ed. C. Mühlegger and B. Schwarzmann-Huter (Innsbruck/Vienna, 1998), 113–126.

8. J. Cocteau, *Journal d'un inconnu* (Grasse, 1952), esp. 13–43 ("De l'invisibilité").

9. See Demisch, *Die Sphinx*, 191–194; S. Brosi, *Der Kuß der Sphinx: Weibliche Gestalten nach griechischem Mythos in Malerei und Graphik des Symbolismus* (Münster,

1993); H. Kimpel and J. Werckmeister, "Die Schöne als das Biest: Zur Ikonographie der Sphinx," in *Don Juan und Femme fatale*, ed. H. H. Kreuzer (Munich, 1994), 117–125; U. Steinmann, *Die Darstellung von Mischwesen in der französischen Kultur des neunzehnten Jahrhunderts am Beispiel der Sphinx* (Diploma Thesis, Vienna, 2000).

10. See H. R. Brittnacher, *Ästhetik des Horrors: Gespenster, Vampire, Monster, Teufel und künstliche Menschen in der phantastischen Literatur* (Frankfurt am Main, 1994), 184f. Such determinations of monstrosity will not be pursued here, rather, see G. Lascault, *Le monstre dans l'art occidentale: Un problème éthique* (Paris, 1973); A. Margalit, "Meanings and Monsters," *Synthese* 44 (1980), 313–346; and esp. H. R. Brittnacher, "Das Monstrum: Zur Ästhetik des Hässlichen; Begriff, Ikonographie, Geschichte," in Brittnacher, *Ästhetik des Horrors*, 183–198.

11. See Brittnacher, *Ästhetik des Horrors*, 185f. and n. 4.

12. Since Cocteau shares this goal with many authors of fantastic literature, his works have been identified as "fantastic" and he himself as a "fantastic writer." For this characterization, see for example, R. Yarrow, "Ambiguity and the Supernatural in Cocteau's *La machine infernale*," in *Staging the Impossible: The Fantastic Mode in Modern Drama*, ed. P. Murphy (London, 1992), 108–115. A key component in this regard is the figure of the threshold, which generally serves as a theme within the genre of the fantastic. See, e.g., U. Wyss, "Jenseits der Schwelle: Die Phantasik der anderen Welt," in *Phantastik — Kult oder Kultur? Aspekte eines Phänomens in Kunst, Literatur und Film*, ed. C. Ivanovic et al. (Stuttgart, 2003), 41–53; J. Lehmann, "Phantastik als Schwellen- und Ambivalenzphänomen," in *Phantastik — Kult oder Kultur?*, ed. Ivanovic, 25–39, esp. 29f.; C. Ivanovic, "Schwellen(w)orte: Phantastik zwischen Affirmation und Subversion," in *Macht und Mythos*, ed. T. Le Blanc and B. Twrsnick (Wetzlar, 2005), 13–36 (= *Schriftenreihe und Materialien der Phantastischen Bibliothek Wetzlar*, vol. 86).

Chapter One

1. See T. Gantz, *Early Greek Myth: A Guide to Literary and Artistic Sources*, vol. 2 (Baltimore, MD, 1993), 467–530 ("Thebes"), esp. 492–502 ("Oidipous").

2. It has been verified that part of the *Oedipodea* depicts the Sphinx devouring, among others, Haimon, the son of Creon. See *Oedipodea* fr. 1 PEG I (= A. Bernabé, ed., *Poetae epici Graeci: Testimonia et fragmenta*, vol. 1 [Leipzig, 1987]) (henceforth Bernabé). Moreover, according to the logic of the saga, the murder of Laius and Oedipus' solving of the Sphinx's riddle must also have belonged to the story. See A. Rzach, "Kyklos," *RE* 11, col. 2347–2435, esp. col. 2358f. (2357–2361: "Oidipodeia").

3. Hom. *Il.* 23.677–680 and *Od.* 11.271–280; Hes. *WD* 162–165; briefly on this matter, see C. Segal, *Oedipus Tyrannus: Tragic Heroism and the Limits of Knowledge* (New York, 1992), 44f.

4. For more on the changes that the Oedipus story underwent in early antiquity and on the development of the version of the myth as we know it today, see E. L. de Kock, "The Sophoklean Oidipus and Its Antecedents," *Acta classica* 4 (1961), 7–28; L. Edmunds, *Oedipus: The Ancient Legend and Its Later Analogues* (Baltimore, 1985); A. Henrichs, "Oidipus," *DNP* 8 (2000), col. 1129–1132; A. Kühr, *Als Kadmos nach Boiotien kam: Polis und Ethnos im Spiegel thebanischer Gründungsmythen* (Stuttgart, 2006), 150–159.

5. There are nine known tragedians who produced a version of the Oedipus drama during this time period. See R. Kannicht, "Ein Hypomnema zum Ödipus des Euripides? P. Vindob. G 29779," *Würzburger Jahrbücher für die Altertumswissenschaft*, n.s. 1 (1975): 71–82, esp. 71n2.

6. On this matter, see de Kock, "The Sophoklean Oidipus and its Antecedents."

7. This summary has been compiled essentially from the depictions in visual art up to the end of the fifth century BCE, the tragic poets, above all Sophocles, and the *Library* of Pseudo-Apollodorus, which appeared many centuries later but made liberal use of the early myth variations. On the images, see: J.-M. Moret, *Œdipe, la Sphinx et les Thebains: Essai de mythologie iconographique*, 2 vols. (Rome, 1984) (henceforth Moret); I. Krauskopf, "Oidipous," *LIMC* 7.1.1–15 (and 7.2.6–15); and N. Kourou, "Sphinx," *LIMC* 7.1.1152–1160. For text segments on Oedipus' life story from birth to death, see in particular Hom. *Od.* 11.273–280; Pind. *O.* 2.38–40; Aesch. *Sept.* 745–757, 772–790; Soph. *OT* 711–723, 774–813, 1237–1279; Soph. *Ant.* 51–54; Soph. *Oid. K.* passim; Eur. *Phoen.* 15–69, 801–817; and Apollod. 3.5.8 (= 3.52–55). On the doom-bringing Sphinx, see, for example, *Oedipodeia* fr. 1 Bernabé; Hes. *Theog.* 326f.; Aesch. *Sept.* 522–524, 539–544; 759f., 776; and Eur. *Phoen.* 806f., 1021f., 1023f., 1760.

8. For more on the history of the many variations of the Sphinx episode, see Gantz, *Early Greek Myth*, 494–498.

9. In other versions of the myth, Oedipus lives on in Thebes, with or without Jocasta (Hom. *Od.* 11.275f.; and Eur. *Phoen.* 59–69), where he dies and is buried (Hom. *Il.* 23,679f.; Aesch. *Sept.* 914, 1004; and Soph. *Ant.* 897–902).

10. Lesky and Herbig, "Sphinx," *RE* 3.A.2, col. 1717; see Athen. 10.456b = Asklepiades *FGrH* 12.F.7a.

11. See Gantz, *Early Greek Myth*, 496.

12. Wolfgang Schadewaldt has thus characterized *Oedipus the King* as a "Drama of Revelation" (*Enthüllungs-Drama*): "Der König Ödipus des Sophokles in neuer Deutung," *Schweizer Monatshefte* 36 (1956), 21–31 (reprinted in Schadewaldt, *Hellas und Hesperien* [Zürich, 1970], 466–476; here, 468).

13. J. Latacz, *Einführung in die griechische Tragödie* (Göttingen, 1993), 162. On tragedy's political function in general and its historical-cultural context, see also W. Rösler, *Polis und Tragödie* (Konstanz, 1980); and C. Meier, *Die politische Kunst der griechischen Tragödie* (Munich, 1988).

14. Soph. *OT* 14–57, esp. (concerning the Sphinx) 33–36 and 52–53.

15. Cf. A. Schmitt, "Menschliches Fehlen und tragisches Scheitern: Zur Handlungsmotivation im Sophokleischen 'König Ödipus,'" *Rheinisches Museum für Philologie* 131 (1988), 8–30, esp. 12–13.

16. Cf. B. Knox, *Oedipus at Thebes* (New Haven, 1957), 53–106 and 107–158, esp. 116–138; Knox, "The Freedom of Oedipus," *New Republic* (Aug. 30, 1982), 28–34; E. Flaig, *Ödipus: Tragischer Vatermord im klassischen Athen* (Munich, 1998); and H. Flashar, *Sophokles: Dichter im demokratischen Athen* (Munich, 2000), 100–122, esp. 118.

17. See, e.g., E. Lefevre, "Die Unfähigkeit, sich zu erkennen: Unzeitgemäße Bemerkungen zu Sophokles' *Oidipous Tyrannos*," *Würzburger Jahrbücher für die Altertumswissenschaft*, n.s. 13 (1987), 37–58; as well as Lefevre, *Die Unfähigkeit, sich*

zu erkennen: Sophokles' Tragödien (Leiden, 2001), 119–147; Schmitt, "Menschliches Fehlen und tragisches Scheitern"; Latacz, *Einführung in die griechische Tragödie*, 235–236; and W. Kullmann, "Die Reaktionen auf die Orakel und ihre Erfüllung im *König Ödipus* des Sophokles," in *Orchestra: Drama, Mythos, Bühne* (Festschrift für H. Flashar), ed. A. Bierl and P. v. Möllendorff (Stuttgart, 1994), 105–118.

18. See, e.g., Segal, *Oedipus Tyrannus*, 103–109.

19. *OT* 300–462. The mixture of self-overestimation and rash emotions, which leads Oedipus to fatal misconduct, is also discernible in the play's restrospective allusions to the murder of Laius. See, e.g., Flashar, "König Ödipus," esp. 114–115. The opposition between Teiresias, who stands in connection with Apollo, and the ruler Oedipus can also be interpreted as one between "mantic authority" and "political authority"; see A. Papaizos, "Autorité mantique et autorité politique: Tirésias et Œdipe," *Kernos* 3 (1990), 307–318. J. Bollack speaks of the opposition between a "political" and a "religious space," *L'Œdipe roi de Sophocle: Le texte et ses interprétations*, vol. 2 (Lille, 1990), 218ff.

20. J. Schmidt, "Sophokles, König Ödipus: Das Scheitern des Aufklärers an der alten Religion," in *Aufklärung und Gegenaufklärung in der europäischen Literatur: Philosophie und Politik von der Antike bis zur Gegenwart*, ed. J. Schmidt (Darmstadt, 1988), 33–55, 41.

21. See also Soph. *OT* 36, 130, 1199, and Eur. *Phoen.* 807 (ἀμουσόταται ᾠδαί). The term ῥαψῳδός is prominent in the scholarship on this topic because the riddle existed in the epic tradition in a hexametric form, and thus, in the fifth century BCE, the Sphinx was seen as a rhapsodist; for more on this, see, for example, Bollack, *L'Oedipe roi de Sophocle*, who writes: "She composes hexameter either as a 'singer,' or as a 'rhapsodist' [s.v. 391], but, in fact, her song dominates the entire lyric register" with "iridescent singing" (s.v. 130). (In German: J. Bollack, *Sophokles, König Ödipus: Übersetzung, Text, Kommentar* [Frankfurt am Main, 1994], 165); H. Flashar, *Sophokles: Dichter im demokratischen Athen* (Munich, 2000), 104.

22. See Sophocles, *Oedipus the King*, trans. D. Grene (Chicago, 2010), 27; Sophocles, *Oedipus the King*, trans. B. Knox (New York, 2005), 24. For further possible translations of γνώμη, see, e.g., T. Halter, *König Oedipus: Von Sophokles zu Cocteau* (Stuttgart, 1998), 126n6.

23. In Soph. *OT* 508, we learn that she is winged; in Soph. *OT* 1199f., that she is a "crooked-taloned oracle-singing girl."

24. See Soph. *OT* 33–36, 52f., 132–134, 440, 510, 1197–1203.

25. See Krauskopf, 7.1.1–18 (and 7.2.6–15); Moret.

26. On this topic, see E. Simon, *Das Satyrspiel Sphinx des Aischylos* (Heidelberg, 1981).

27. Attic red-figured krater, Lecce, Museo Provinciale 610, c. 470/460 BCE, Oedipus, bearded, with cane and himation; Sphinx on a short Ionian column; on the reverse side, a satyr. Moret, no. 69, table 39.2.3.

28. Attic red-figured *kylix* with Sphinx riddle (interior decoration), Vatican, Museo Gregoriano Etrusco 16541 (from Vulci), c. 480/470 BCE, Oedipus bearded, with *chlamys, petasus*, and shoes; Sphinx on a short Ionian column; on the reverse side, a satyr scene. Moret, no. 87, table 50, 51.1. This vase painting is discussed in broader context by E. C. Keuls, *Painter and Poet in Ancient Greece: Iconography and*

the Literary Arts (Stuttgart, 1997), 402, fig. 54; J. Boardman, *The History of Greek Vases: Potters, Painters and Pictures* (London, 2001), 196, fig. 212; T. Petit, *Œdipe et le Cherubin: Les sphinx levantins, cypriotes et grecs comme gardiens d'Immortalité* (Fribourg, 2011), fig. 1-2; K. Junker, *Interpreting the Images of Greek Myths: An Introduction* (Cambridge, 2012), 23, fig. 8.

29. An inscription runs around the rim of the interior decoration, giving the name of the hero Oedipus (not visible in the reproduction but seen in the upper left of the original). The two words [κ]αι τρι[πουν] are seen directly between the heads of the two figures. Although the mouth of the Sphinx is clearly closed, these words form part of the riddle she is posing. The fact that the riddle scene is combined with images of satyrs on these vessels supports the thesis that Aeschylus' satyr-play *Sphinx* pushed Oedipus into the central heroic role in the larger story of how Thebes was menaced by the Sphinx. A depiction on a *hydria* from the Fujita private collection, dating likewise from 470/460 and showing white-haired satyrs before the Sphinx, lends further support. The satyrs, undauntedly examining the Sphinx, seem here to have taken on the role of old-fashioned Theban dignitaries: attic red-figured *hydria*, private collection Fujita (at the time of writing on loan in the Martin von Wagner Museum, University of Würzburg), c. 470/460 BCE, satyrs, festively attired, sitting in fine armchairs. The Sphinx crouches across from them, on a cliff. Moret, no. 188, table 90.

30. For intellectual-historical context, see B. M. W. Knox, *Oedipus at Thebes* (New Haven, 1957), 53–106 and 107–158 ("Athens" and "Man"), esp. 124–138 (on γνώμη and related terminology); V. di Benedetto, *Sofocle* (Florence, 1983), 85–104 ("Edipo: La crisi delle strutture intelettuali"); C. Meier, *Die Entstehung einer autonomen Intelligenz bei den Griechen*, in *Kulturen der Achsenzeit*, ed. S. N. Eisenstadt (Frankfurt am Main, 1987), pt. 1, pp. 89–127. For more on the hero based on mental rather than physical power, see also J. P. Wilson, *The Hero and the City: An Interpretation of Sophocles' Oedipus at Colonus* (Ann Arbor, 1997), 178n17.

31. See also Lefèvre, "Die Unfähigkeit, sich zu erkennen," esp. 43–47.

32. A. Lesky, *Die tragische Dichtung der Hellenen* (Göttingen, 1972), 221.

33. See, for example, M. Lurje, *Die Suche nach der Schuld: Sophokles' Oedipus Rex, Aristoteles' Poetik und das Tragödienverständnis der Neuzeit* (Munich, 2004).

34. Cf. K. Reinhardt, *Sophokles* (Frankfurt am Main, 1933), 104–144 ("Oedipus Tyrannus"), esp. 143f. Comparable standpoints are represented by, among others, K. von Fritz, *Antike und moderne Tragödie: Neun Abhandlungen* (Berlin, 1962), 14; and T. Gould, "The Innocence of Oedipus: The Philosophers on Oedipus the King," *Arion* 4 (1965), 363–386, 582–611; and *Arion* 5 (1966), 478–525.

35. W. Schadewaldt, *Sophokles und das Leid* (Potsdam, 1944); reprinted in Schadewaldt, *Hellas und Hesperien*, 385–401; Schadewaldt, "Der König Oedipus," 21–31; reprinted in *Hellas und Hesperien*, 466–476, here 473.

36. W. Kullmann, "Die Reaktionen auf die Orakel und ihre Erfüllung im *König Ödipus* des Sophokles," in *Orchestra: Drama, Mythos, Bühne*, ed. A. Bierl and P. von Möllendorff (Festschrift für H. Flashar) (Stuttgart, 1994), 105–118, here 106.

37. *OT* 1524–1530 (trans. R. Jebb). The possibility that this verse, in the form that it was supposedly recited, may have been an inauthentic conclusion to the story—as R. D. Dawe argues in "On Interpolations in the Two Oedipus Plays of

Sophocles," *Rheinisches Museum für Philologie* 144 (2001), 1–21—changes nothing here. These lines contain authentic Greek wisdom; their admonitory function is clear. The thoughts expressed here appear similarly in Aesch. *Ag.* 928f.; Soph. *Trach.* 1–3; Eur. *Tro.* 509f., Heraclitus 865f.; Andr. 100–102. For more on the discussion about the tragedy's conclusion, see H. Lloyd-Jones and N. G. Wilson, *Sophoclea: Studies in the Text of Sophocles* (Oxford, 1990), 113f.; and J. Bollack, *L'Oedipe roi de Sophocle: Le texte et ses interprétations*(Lille, 1990), 4:1038–1045; C. W. Müller, "Die thebanische Trilogie des Sophokles und ihre Aufführung im Jahre 401: Zur Frühgeschichte der antiken Sophokles Rezeption und der Überlieferung des Textes," *Rheinisches Museum für Philologie* 139 (1996), 193–224, esp. 218–221.

    38. On this matter, see K. Töchterle, *Lucius Annaeus Seneca: Oedipus: Kommentar mit Einleitung, Text und Übersetzung* (Heidelberg, 1994), 9–22; W. Kofler and M. Korenjak, "Der literarische Ödipus: Ein Streifzug von der Antike bis Cocteau," in *Resonanzen: Innsbrucker Beiträge zum modernen Musiktheater bei den Salzburger Festspielen*, ed. C. Mühlegger and B. Schwarzmann-Huter (Innsbruck, 1998), 59–83, esp. 66–68. On the Sphinx episode's function as a generator of threatening undertones, see V. Wurnig, *Gestaltung und Funktion von Gefühlsdarstellungen in den Tragödien Senecas: Interpretationen zu einer Technik der dramatischen Stimmungserzeugung* (Frankfurt am Main, 1982), 22f.

    39. See Hom. *Od.* 12.39–54 (Circe's description), esp. 41–46; see A.-B. Renger, *Zwischen Märchen und Mythos: Die Abenteuer des Odysseus und andere Geschichten von Homer bis Walter Benjamin: Eine gattungstheoretische Studie* (Stuttgart, 2006), 268–270.

    40. Sen. *Oed.* 92–102: "nec Sphinga caecis verba nectentem modis / fugi: cruentos vatis infandae tuli / rictus et albens ossibus sparsis solum; / cumque e superna rupe iam praedae imminens / aptaret alas verbera et caudae movens / saevi leonis more conciperet minas, / carmen poposci: sonuit horrendum insuper, / crepuere malae, saxaque impatiens morae / revulsit unguis viscera expectans mea; / nodosa sortis verba et implexos dolos / ac triste carmen alitis solvi ferae." "Even when facing the Sphinx, who strings her words together in the darkest of ways, I did not flee. I have defied the bloody vengeance of that ghastly seer, and stood upright upon the ground, shimmering white with strewn bones; and as she shouted out threats like a fierce lion, her wings outstretched at the ready, the whip of her tail in motion, lying in wait to ambush her prey from atop the high cliff, there and then did I demand to hear her riddle: nightmarishly did she let it resound above me, her jaws gnashing, and, suffering no hesitation, tore her claws from the cliff, slavering for my innards. I unraveled the serpentine words and all of the interwoven guile of the doom pronouncement of the winged beast, to find the hidden solution."

    41. Gérard Genette, *Palimpsests: Literature in the Second Degree*, trans. C. Newman and C. Doubinsky (Lincoln, 1997).

    42. Quite a number of studies have appeared on this theme. Especially helpful among them are W. Brach, *Der Œdipe von Corneille und der des Voltaire, verglichen mit dem Oedipus Rex des Sophokles* (Diss., Marburg an der Lahn, 1914); W. Jördens, *Die französischen Ödipusdramen: Ein Beitrag zum Fortleben der Antike und zur Geschichte der französischen Tragödie* (Bochum, 1933); M. Mueller, *Children of Oedipus and other Essays on the Imitation of Greek Tragedy, 1550–1800* (Toronto, 1980), 105–152. A short,

summary rendering (of Sophocles, Seneca, medieval sources, Corneille, Voltaire, Platen, Hofmannsthal, and Cocteau) can be found in W. Kofler and M. Korenjak, "Der literarische Ödipus: Ein Streifzug von der Antike bis Cocteau," 70–73. On Corneille's treatment of this material, the following are recommended: W. H. Friedrich, "Ein Ödipus mit gutem Gewissen: Über Corneilles Œdipe," in Friedrich, *Vorbild und Neugestaltung: Sechs Kapitel zur Geschichte der Tragödie* (Göttingen, 1967), 112–139; P. A. Ogundele, "The Oedipus Story in the Hands of Sophocles, Seneca and Corneille," *Nigeria and the Classics* 12 (1970), 31–51; on Voltaire's treatment: P. Vidal-Naquet, "Œdipe à Vicence et à Paris: Deux moments d'une histoire," *Quaderni di storia* 14 (1981), 3–21 (ANOVA compare with other editions of the eighteenth century).

43. *Œdipe* 247f.; quoted from Corneille, *Œuvres complètes* (Bibliothèque de la Pléiade): *Textes établis, présentés et annotés*, ed. G. Couton (Paris, 1987), vol. 3, 13–93 (*Œdipe*), here 31.

44. The scholarship has comprehensively investigated the comparisons to be drawn between *Oedipus the King* and *La machine infernale* in terms of repeated structures and content. See, for example, G. Mason, "La Machine Infernale: A Modern Adaptation of the Oedipus Legend by Jean Cocteau," *Greece & Rome* 9.27 (1940), 178–187, esp. 183–187; L. W. Leadbeater, "In Defense of Cocteau: Another View of *La machine infernale*," *Classical and Modern Literature* 10.2 (1990), 113–125; H. D. Page, "The resurrection of the Sophoclean Phoenix: Jean Cocteau's *La machine infernale*," *Classical and Modern Literature* 18.4 (1998), 329–343.

Chapter Two

1. A. Lesky and R. Herbig, "Sphinx," *RE* 3.A.2, col. 1703–1749, here 1711.

2. L. W. Daly, "Oedipus," *RE* 17, col. 2103–2117 and *RE* Suppl. 7, col. 769–786, here col. 786; see also L. Deubner, *Oedipusprobleme* (Berlin, 1942). For an overview of this and other interpretations of the "Oedipus-form," see W. Pötscher, "Die Oidipus-Gestalt," in Pötscher, *Hellas und Rom* (Hildesheim, 1988), 237–272.

3. Cf. C. Robert, *Oidipus: Geschichte eines poetischen Stoffes im Altertum*, vol. 1 (Berlin, 1915).

4. Cf. M. P. Nilsson, "Der Oidipusmythos," *Göttingische Gelehrte Anzeigen* 184 (1922), 36–46.

5. See, for example, U. Hausmann, "Oidipus und die Sphinx," *Jahrbuch der staatlichen Kunstsammlungen in Baden-Württemberg* 9 (1972), 7–36.

6. V. Propp, "Edip v svete fol'klora," *Ucenye zapiski Leningradskogo Gosudarstvennogo Universiteta / Serija filologiceskich nauk* 9.72 (1944): 138–175 (= "Oedipus in the Light of Folklore," in *Oedipus: A Folklore Casebook*, ed. L. Edmunds and A. Dundes (New York, 1983), 76–121.

7. L. Edmunds, *The Sphinx in the Oedipus Legend* (= *Beiträge zur klassischen Philologie* 127) (Königstein, Ts., 1981), 1.

8. The essay, originally in English, appeared in 1955 in T. A. Sebeok, ed., *Myth: A Symposium* (Bibliographical and Special Series of the American Folklore Society, vol. 5) (Philadelphia, 1955), 428–444. Three years later, Lévi-Strauss incorporated the essay into his *Anthropologie structurale* (Paris, 1958), 227–255, in his own translation, under the title "La structure des mythes," with the proviso "Traduit avec quelques compléments et modifications."

9. See C. Calame, "Le nom d'Œdipe," in *Edipo: Il teatro greco e la cultura europea*, ed. B. Gentili and R. Pretagostini (Rome, 1986), 395–407.

10. See Soph. *OT* 1032ff.; Eur. *Phoen.* 26f.; Diodorus Siculus 4.64.1; Apollod. 3.5.7 (= 3.49).

11. W. Benjamin, *Das Passagen-Werk*, 2 vols., R. Tiedemann, ed. (Frankfurt am Main, 1983), 1:618; *The Arcades Project*, trans. H. Eiland and K. McLaughlin, (Cambridge, Mass., 1999), 494 (translation modified).

12. A. van Gennep, *The Rites of Passage* (in French, *Les rites de passage*, 1909; London, 1960).

13. L. Gernet and A. Boilanger, *Le génie grec dans la religion* (Paris, 1932); M. Delcourt, ed., *Œdipe ou la légende du conquérant* (1944; Paris, 1981); V. Propp, "Oedipus in the Light of Folklore."

14. J. Bremmer, "Oedipus and the Greek Oedipus Complex," in *Interpretations of Greek Mythology*, ed. Bremmer (London, 1987), 41–59. According to Bremmer, the structure of the Oedipus story corresponds to the structure of the Theseus story, in Greek mythology, and the story of Geriguiguiatugo, in South American mythology. In each case, he takes the structure of the story to be an example of a familiar story type, in which a young man commits an impressive act of heroism, vanquishes a monster, kills his father (or causes his death), and becomes king (or a culture hero). According to Bremmer, the meaning of the Oedipus story in the context of archaic Greece, where parricide was among the most heinous of all crimes, is simple: the myth can be read as a warning to the younger generation, to remember that adulthood demands deference to one's fathers. Bremmer regards the incest motif as a late addition to the myth. In fifth-century BCE Athens—judging from how Sophocles contrived his version of the Oedipus myth— there was a particular significance associated with parricide: it highlighted the strict segregation at that time of women and young men from elder men, who, especially in families of high standing, were not allowed to sustain close relationships even with their fathers. In light of this, Bremmer sees ample cause for drawing connections between murdering the father and committing incest with the mother, which he sees as the lynchpin of Sophocles' tragedy.

15. Van Gennep, *The Rites of Passage*, 18.

16. Ibid., 18–19.

17. A. van Gennep, ibid., 19–25.

18. See V. Turner, "Betwixt and Between: The Liminal Period in *Rites of Passage*," in Turner, *The Forest of Symbols: Aspects of Ndembu Ritual* (Ithaca, 1967), 93–111; Turner, *The Ritual Process: Structure and Anti-Structure* (1969, repr. New York, 1995, esp. 94–111.

19. V. Turner, *The Ritual Process*, 95.

20. Van Gennep, *The Rites of Passage*, 21–22. On the topic, see also N. Ritter, "Die andere Sphinx—Torwächter und Schutzwesen in Assyrien," in *Wege der Sphinx— Monster zwischen Orient und Okzident*, ed. L. Winkler-Horaček (Rahden, Westphalia., 2011), 67–76.

21. On this development, see Winkler-Horaček, *Wege der Sphinx*.

22. On the Egyptian Sphinx, see H. Demisch, *Die Sphinx: Geschichte ihrer Darstellung von den Anfängen bis zur Gegenwart* (Stuttgart, 1977), 16–39; and U. Dubiel,

"Pharao—Gott—Wächter: Sphingen im Alten Ägypten," in Winkler-Horaček, *Wege der Sphinx*, 5–25.

23. On the Sphinx in the Middle East and on Crete, see Demisch, *Die Sphinx*, 40–63 and 64–75; and L. Winkler-Horačk, "Wege der Sphinx: Von Ägypten und Vorderasien nach Griechenland," in Winkler-Horaček, *Wege der Sphinx*, 99–115.

24. See N. Kourou, "Sphinx," *LIMC* 7.1.1152–1160.

25. See I. Krauskopf, "Oidipous," *LIMC* 7.1.3–9; Kourou, "Sphinx," *LIMC* 7.1.116of.; L. Winkler-Horaček, "Der geflügelte Menschenlöwe (Sphinx): Ein Bildmotiv der frühgriechischen Vasenmalerei und sein Verhältnis zu den östlichen Vorbildern," in *Griechische Keramik im kulturellen Kontext: Akten des Internationalen Vasen-Symposions in Kiel vom 24. bis 28.9.2001*, ed. B. Schmaltz and M. Söldner (Münster, 2003), 225–228; U. Höckmann and L. Winkler-Horaček, "Sphinx im frühen Griechenland und thebanische Sphinx (Kat 30–37)," in *Ägypten—Griechenland—Rom: Abwehr und Berührung*. Städelsches Kunstinstitut und Städtische Galerie. [Exhibition from November 26, 2005 until February 26, 2006], ed. H. Beck and P. Bol (Tübingen, 2005), 90–96, 477–483; L. Winkler-Horaček, "Vom Bild zum Mythos, vom Mythos zum Bild: Der 'geflügelte Menschenlöwe' und die Sphinx von Theben," in *Wege der Sphinx*, 163–166.

26. See Demisch, *Die Sphinx*, 83–88.

27. Eur. *Phoen.* 806.

28. Apollod. 5.5.8 (= 3.52). See also schol. Eur. *Phoen.* 45.

29. Diod. 4.64.3: καθ' ὃν δὴ χρόνον μυθολογοῦσι σφίγγα, δίμορφον θηρίον, παραγενομένην εἰς τὰς Θήβας αἴνιγμα προτιθέναι τῷ δυναμένῳ λῦσαι, καὶ πολλοὺς ὑπ' αὐτῆς δι' ἀπορίαν ἀναιρεῖσθαι. "At the same time—so the myth was told—a Sphinx, a double-formed abomination, is said to have come to Thebes, and to have presented a riddle to any and all who believed they could solve it, and she is said to have killed many who were not up to the task."

30. For genealogical variants beyond those mentioned here, see J. Ilberg, "Sphinx," in *Ausführliches Lexikon der griechischen und römischen Mythologie*, ed. W. H. Roscher (henceforth *Roscher*), vol. 4, col. 1298–1409, here col. 1364.

31. Apollod. 3.5.8 (= 3.52); Hyg. *Fab. praef.* 39.

32. Echidna was the mother of numerous other monstrous figures: among them, stemming from her congress with Typhon—according to Hes. *Theog.* 306–325—were the two-headed dog Orthos, the fifty-headed hellhound Cerberus, the nine-headed Hydra, also known as the "Lernaean Snake," and the three-headed Chimaera. The slaying of such monsters was a favorite theme of archaic art.

33. Schol. Hes. *Theog.* 326.

34. Hes. *Theog.* 326f.; According to Hesiod, Orthos also sired the Nemean Lion with Echidna (327–332).

35. Eur. *Phoen.* 1023; Hdt. 4.9.1.

36. Eur. *Phoen.* 810f.: γένναν, ἂν ὁ κατὰ χθονὸς Ἅιδας Καδμείοις ἐπιπέμπει—"who Hades sent from hell"; 1019–1025: ὢ πτερούσσα, γᾶς λόχευμα / νερτέρου τ' Ἐχίδνας, / Καδμείων ἁρπαγά, /πολύφθορος πολύστονος / μειξοπάρθενος, δάιον τέρας, / φοιτάσι πτεροῖς / χαλαῖσί τ' ὠμοσίτοις—"O winged one, child of the earth / and from the downcast Echidna line / robber of Cadmus' clan; / rich in death, rich in suffering, /

half animal, half girl, / ill-boding monster, / with wild wings, / and claws that rip at the flesh of men."

37. Cf. J.-P. Vernant, *Les origines de la pensée grecque* (Paris, 1962); in English, *The Origins of Greek Thought* (Ithaca, NY, 1982), 102–118 ("Cosmogonies and Myths of Sovereignty"), esp. 105–110; Vernant, *Mythe et société en Grèce ancienne* (Paris, 1981); in English, *Myth and Society in Ancient Greece* (Atlantic Highlands, NJ, 1980; repr. New York, 1988), 101–119 ("The Society of the Gods").

38. Hes. *Theog.* 297–300.

39. Ibid., 304 (see Hom. *Il.* 2.783); Hdt. 4.8f.; Aristoph. *Ran.* 473.

40. On the positioning of hybrid creatures on the borders of the world, see also L. Winkler-Horaček, "Fiktionale Grenzräume im Frühen Griechenland," in *Mensch und Tier in der Antike — Grenzziehung und Grenzüberschreitung* (= records of the international classics conference at the University of Rostock, from April 7–9, 2005), ed. A. Alexandridis, M. Wild, and L. Winkler-Horaček (Wiesbaden, 2008), 493–515; H. Schade, *Dämonen und Monstren: Gestaltungen des Bösen in der frühen Kunst des Mittelalters* (Regensburg, 1962), 37.

41. Aeschylus, based on Aristoph. *Ran.* 1287; Soph. *OT* 391.

42. Cf. M. Lurker, "Hund und Wolf in ihrer Beziehung zum Tode," *Antaios* 10 (1968/1969): 199–216; Lurker, "Der Hund als Symboltier für den Übergang vom Diesseits in das Jenseits," *Zeitschrift für Religions- und Geistesgeschichte* 35 (1983), 132–144.

43. Palaephatus 4.

44. See H. Walter, "Sphingen," *Antike und Abendland* 9 (1960): 60–72, esp. 63–69.

45. Aesch. *Sept.* 776: τὰν ἁρπαξάνδραν / κῆρ᾽ For more on archaeological testaments, see Demisch, *Die Sphinx*, 83–85.

46. Eur. *Phoen.* 806; Paus. 9.26.2.

47. In 9.2.4, Pausanias referred to the Kithara Mountains as Oedipus' place of banishment; thus it is the very same mountain range — on the outskirts of Thebes — where the Sphinx resides, and where Oedipus was exposed.

48. Apollod. 3.5.8 (= 3.52); schol. Hes. *Theog.* 326.

49. Cf. Lesky and Herbig, "Sphinx," *RE* 3.A.2, col. 1703–1749, esp. col. 1703, 1709, 1715.

50. Hes. *Theog.* 326 (Phix as a threat to Thebes).

51. Lycoph. 1465; see also schol. Lycoph. 1465, where the winged lion-woman who sits on Φίκιον ὄρος is extensively discussed with regard to, among other factors, Euripides' description of the Sphinx as τέρας (Eur. *Phoen.* 806).

52. Strab. 9.2.34.

53. Cf. van Gennep, *The Rites of Passage*, 18. The marketplace (Greek: ἀγορά), in the topographic sense, was the political, religious, social, and economic center of the Greek polis, demarcated as a sacred district.

54. For more on variants, see A. Lesky and R. Herbig, "Sphinx," *RE* 3.A.2, col. 1703–1749, esp. col. 1715f.; T. Gantz, *Early Greek Myth*, 495–498.

55. For more on the mytho-topography of the gates of Thebes, see A. Kühr, *Als Kadmos nach Boiotien kam: Polis und Ethnos im Spiegel thebanischer Gründungsmythen* (Stuttgart, 2006), 209–219.

56. Van Gennep, *The Rites of Passage*, 20–21.

57. Hom. *Il.* 14.319f.; Hes. *Theog.* 280–283; (Pseud.) Hes. *Scut.* 222–234; Sim. *PMG* fr. 543; see also Pherecydes *FGrH* 3.F.10–12 with Apollod. 2.4.1–2, 4, 5 (= 2.34–49). Pindar details the myth in its most extensive form (*P.* 10.31–50); fragments of what has been handed down indicate that the attic tragedians also took it up (citations in L. Käppel and B. Bäbler, "Perseus," *DNP* 9, col. 612–614, esp. col. 612f.: "I. Mythologie"). With the Romans, see, among others, Ov. *Met.* 4.610–803; 5.1–249; Hyg. *Fab.* 63f. Perseus' advantage over Oedipus was that Athena gave him a radiant shield that had the ability to show his opponents their own reflections, and thereby protected him from having to look them directly in the eye (and thus the Gorgon was killed by her own deadly visage); see J.-P. Vernant, "Death in the Eyes: Gorgo, Figure of the *Other*," in Vernant, *Mortals and Immortals: Collected Essays* (Princeton, NJ, 1992), 11–168, esp. 134–138; T. Macho, "Narziß und der Spiegel: Selbstrepräsentation in der Geschichte der Optik," in *Narcissus: Ein Mythos von der Antike bis zum Cyberspace*, ed. A.-B. Renger (Stuttgart, 2002), 13–25, esp. 18–20 ("Spiegel und Waffe: *Perseus*").

58. See Hom. *Il.* 6.152–205, esp. 179ff.; Hes. *Theog.* 319ff.; Apollod. 2.3.1 (= 2.30). Incidentally, Bellerophon was said to have killed the Chimaera in Lycia, on the edge of the Greek world, and, furthermore, to have triumphed—in each case with the help of the winged horse Pegasus—over the rapacious, non-Greek Solymoi, as well as the Amazons, all equally representative of disturbance in the social order. According to Pindar *O.* 13.69, Poseidon helped Bellerophon to restrain the divine horse Pegasus. Homer does not mention Pegasus, but in other sources he is consistently connected with Bellerophon's victories (Hes. *Theog.* 325; Pind. *O.* 13.87).

59. Theseus' journey to Crete and his slaying of the Minotaur is his most renowned deed. But the Athenian national hero proved himself through numerous other deeds as well, many of which contributed toward overcoming actual or possible disturbances in the world order (Bacchyl. 18.19–30; complete Diod. 4.59.2–5; Apollod. 3.217f. (= 3.16.1); Plut. *Theseus = Th.* 8–11). Even before he came to sovereignty, he killed numerous robbers on his way to Athens, and defeated both the Crommyonian Sow, who had claimed many lives, and the giant Procrustes. After his arrival in Athens, he rendered outstanding services to the land by bringing down the Marathonian Bull, which, according to Isocr. *Or.* 10.25 was sent by Poseidon, or, according to Apollod. 2.95 (= 2.5.7) was the Cretan Bull slain by Hercules. Later, when Theseus had already assumed sovereignty over Attica (and ruled wisely), he fought alongside Hercules against the Amazons (Eur. *Heraclid.* 215–217) when they bore down upon Attica, finally defeating them (Isocr. *Or.* 12.193; Diod. 4.28.1–4; Apollod. *Epit.* 1.16). Furthermore, he helped Pirithous, King of the Lapiths, to chase away the Centaurs, who tried to steal his wives on his wedding night (Isocr. *Or.* 10.26; Diod. 4.70.3).

60. Soph. *OT* 1199f.; see also Lycoph. 1465f., where the oracle Cassandra is compared with the monster of Phikion in terms of their common usage of dark-sounding, confusing words.

61. See J.-P. Vernant, "Ambiguïté et renversement: Sur la structure énigmatique d'Œdipe-roi," in *Mythe et tragédie en Grèce ancienne*, ed. Vernant and P. Vidal-Naquet (Paris, 1973), 99–132; in English, "Ambiguity and Reversal: On the

Enigmatic Structure of *Oedipus Rex*," in *Myth and Tragedy in Ancient Greece*, trans. J. Lloyd, (New York/ Cambridge, 1988), 113–140.

62. J.-P. Vernant, "Ambiguity and Reversal," 116.

63. Ibid., 131.

64. M. Delcourt drew connections between the Oedipus figure and the scapegoat ritual in his *Légendes et cultes de héros en Grèce* (Paris, 1942). The scapegoat theories of Vernant and René Girard (the latter of whom set out a theory, in his 1972 *La violence et le sacré*, referencing Oedipus among other figures, that one can replace the social-integrative function of this practice qua mimesis in theater, as soon as it has gotten into the circle) have been discussed within debates on the context of religion and literature. For more on this, see A. Bierl, "Literatur und Religion als Rito- und Mythopoetik: Überblicksartikel zu einem neuen Ansatz in der Klassischen Philologie," in *Literatur und Religion 1: Wege zu einer mythisch-rituellen Poetik bei den Griechen*, ed. A. Bierl, R. Lämmle and K. Wesselmann (Berlin, 2007), 1–76, esp. 33–36 (see also Bierl, "Religion und Literatur," in *DNP* 15.2 [2002]: col. 669–677). It would collapse the already broadly extended framework of the present discussion to go any further into this. We will thus refrain from considering whether the drama was a ritual or whether it made use of ritual—that is, whether its structure was based on the scapegoat ritual or any other *rite de passage* ritual, in part or in full. Let us clearly establish, however, that the Oedipus story unquestionably depicted a transition that had to be consummated and, as such, that it is programmed by quasi-inherited pre- and extraliterary narrative structures and underlying structures, just as they occur also in rites of passage, as guidelines and controlling factors en route to consummated transitions. Second, let us establish that Sophocles' dramatic depiction of Oedipus' as a transition story, just like rites of passage, is a permutation of this structure.

65. Vernant, "Ambiguity and Reversal," 116.

66. See this short entry in Apollod. 3.5.8 (= 3.55): ἡ μὲν οὖν Σφὶγξ πὸ τῆς κροπόλεως ἑαυτὴν ἔρριψεν, Οἰδίπους δὲ καὶ τὴν βασιλείαν παρέλαβε καὶ τὴν μητέρα ἔγημεν γνοῶν, καὶ παῖδας ἐτέκνωσεν ἐξ αὑτῆς Πολυνείκη καὶ Ἐτεοκλέα, θυγατέρας δὲ Ἰσμήνην καὶ Ἀντιγόνην. "And now the Sphinx threw herself down from her high perch; but Oedipus took over sovereignty, and, without knowing it, married his mother and, as sons, begot Polynices and Eteocles with her, and, as daughters, Ismene and Antigone."

67. *Oinochoe*, fr., red-figure, Berlin, Staatliche Museen V.I. 3186, 450/440 BCE, Sphinx exaggeratedly shown as a hybrid creature with a beard on a cliff, Oedipus with the lower body of a dog. Moret, no. 196, table 96.2.

68. Sen. *Oed.* 638–641.

69. See also the interpretations of F. I. Zeitlin, "Thebes: Theater of Self and Society in Athenian Drama," in *Nothing to Do with Dionysos? Athenian Drama in Its Social Context*, ed. J. J. Winkler and F. I. Zeitlin (Princeton, 1990), 130–167, esp. 154; J.-P. Vernant, *Entre mythe et politique* (Paris, 1996), 331; J. P. Wilson, *The Hero and the City: An Interpretation of Sophocles' Oedipus at Colonus* (Ann Arbor, 1997), 12f.; E. Flaig, *Ödipus: Tragischer Vatermord im klassischen Athen* (Munich, 1998), 93f.

70. Soph. *OT* 96–98 (Apollo), 228f., 236–243 (Oedipus), 417–419, 454–456 (Teiresias).

71. The fact that Oedipus would soon be up in the Kithara Mountains is one of Teiresias' many pronouncements that Oedipus ignored during their argument; see *OT* 421.

72. Soph. *OT* 1451–1454, 1518f. On the question of exile, also with regard to *Oedipus at Colonus*, see B. Seidensticker, "Beziehungen zwischen den beiden Oidipusdramen des Sophokles," in *Hermes* 100 (1972), 255–274; R. D. Dawe, "On Interpolations in the Two Oedipus Plays of Sophocles," *Rheinisches Museum für Philologie* 144 (2001), 1–21.

73. We know from the works received from Sophocles and Euripides that both thoroughly appreciated the cultural advancement of man, but at the same time warned against the ambivalence that came with the freedom inherent within this advancement. They warned against ingratitude and hubris against the gods, who still required thanksgiving, and thus they warned against possible downfall. For more on this topic, see Soph. *Ant.* 332–375; Eur. *Suppl.* 195–218.

Chapter Three

1. Cf., e.g., B. Eschenburg and H. Friedel, eds., *Der Kampf der Geschlechter: Der neue Mythos in der Kunst 1850–1930*, Exhibition Catalogue (Munich, 1995).

2. There is a wealth of studies on the portrayal of feminine threat in literature and art around 1900. Particularly recommended as general surveys are B. Dijkstra, *Idols of Perversity: Fantasies of Feminine Evil in Fin-de-Siècle Culture* (New York, 1986), esp. "Poison Flowers: Maenads of the Decadence and the Torrid Wail of the Sirens," 235–271, and "Gynanders and Genetics: Connoisseurs of Bestiality and Serpentine Delight; Leda, Circe, and the Cold Caresses of the Sphinx," 272–332; C. Hilmes, "Sehnsucht nach Erlösung: Bilder des Weiblichen um 1900," in *Ästhetische und religiöse Erfahrungen der Jahrhundertwenden*, ed. W. Braungart (Paderborn, 1998), 276–289; and B. Pohle, *Kunstwerk Frau: Inszenierungen von Weiblichkeit in der Moderne* (Frankfurt am Main, 1998).

3. See, e.g., J. Sayers, *Mothers of Psychoanalysis: Helene Deutsch, Karen Horney, Anna Freud, Melanie Klein* (New York, 1991). Whereas Freud proposed that the father (paternal phallus) was central to infantile and adult psychosexual development, Klein focused more on the early relationship with the mother, insisting that Oedipal manifestations are perceptible in the first year of life, the oral stage. Her insistence became a feature of the so-called "Controversial Discussions" which took place in the British Psychoanalytical Association between 1942 and 1944. Karen Horney too reworked the Freud's Oedipal complex of the sexual elements, claiming that the clinging to one parent and jealousy of the other was simply the result of anxiety, caused by a disturbance in the parent-child relationship. Regarding Freud's notion of "penis envy," she suggested that it is men who are adversely affected by their inability to bear children, which she referred to as "womb envy." Her challenge to Freud's theories, along with that of Melanie Klein, produced the first psychoanalytic debate on femininity. On Karen Horney see J. L. Rubins, *Karen Horney: Gentle Rebel of Psychoanalysis* (New York, 1978); S. Quinn, *A Mind of Her Own: The Life of Karen Horney* (New York, 1987); S. T. Hitchcock, *Karen Horney: Pioneer of Feminine Psychology* (Philadelphia, 2005). On Melanie Klein see H. Segal, *Melanie Klein* (New York, 1979); P. Grosskurth, *Melanie Klein: Her World and Her Work* (New

York, 1986); Julia Kristeva, *Melanie Klein* (European Perspectives: A Series in Social Thought and Cultural Criticism) (New York, 2004).

4. Cf., e.g. K. Flaake, "Psychoanalyse," in *Gender-Studien: eine Einführung*, ed. C. von Braun and I. Stephan (Stuttgart, 2000), 169–179.

5. Cf. S. de Beauvoir, *The Second Sex* (1949; New York, 1989).

6. Cf., e.g., R. Schlesier, *Konstruktionen der Weiblichkeit bei Sigmund Freud: Zum Problem von Entmythologisierung und Remythologisierung in der psychoanalytischen Theorie* (Frankfurt am Main, 1981), 165–172; and R. Vogt, *Psychoanalyse zwischen Mythos und Aufklärung oder das Rätsel der Sphinx* (Frankfurt am Main, 1989), 105–154.

7. S. Freud, "Femininity," lecture 33 in *New Introductory Lectures on Psycho-Analysis, SE* 22: 112–136; S. Freud, "Die Weiblichkeit," in *Neue Folge der Vorlesungen zur Einführung in die Psychoanalyse* (1933) in *Gesammelte Werke*, ed. Anna Freud et al., with the participation of Marie Bonaparte (London, 1940) (henceforth, *GW*), 15:119–145, here 120 (*SE* 22: 113).

8. S. Freud, "Über die weibliche Sexualität" (1931): *GW* 14: 517–537, here 522 and 526 [*SE* 21: 225–246, here 230 and 234–35], here 522 and 526. On "penis-envy," see also Freud, "Die Weiblichkeit," *GW* 15:119–145, here 134 [*SE* 22: 112–136, here 127].

9. S. Freud, "Die Weiblichkeit," *GW* 15:119–145, here 134 [*SE* 22: 112–136, here 127].

10. Cf., e.g., I. Stephan, "Im Zeichen der Sphinx. Psychoanalytischer und literarischer Diskurs über Weiblichkeit um 1900," in Stephan, *Musen & Medusen: Mythos und Geschlecht in der Literatur des 20. Jahrhunderts* (Cologne/Weimar/Vienna, 1997), 14–36, esp. 17–19; and R. Vogt, *Psychoanalyse zwischen Mythos und Aufklärung*, 104–126.

11. Cf. M. Foucault's introduction to L. Binswanger, *Traum und Existenz* (Bern/Berlin, 1992), 7–93 (Foucault translated Binswanger's *Dream and Existence* from German into French and added a substantial essay-introduction which highlighted the necessity of "steeping oneself in the manifest content of the dream.")

12. S. Freud, *Die Traumdeutung* (1900), in *GW* (London 1942), 2/3:1–626, here 269. The translation is from *The Interpretation of Dreams*, trans. J. Crick (Oxford, 1999), 202. Subsequent translations from the *Traumdeutung* are taken from this edition.

13. See R. Schlesier, "Auf den Spuren von Freuds Ödipus," in *Antike Mythen in der europäischen Tradition*, ed. H. Hofmann (Tübingen, 1999), 281–300, esp. 282f.

14. S. Freud, *Briefe an Wilhelm Fliess 1887–1904: Ungekürzte Ausgabe*, ed. J. M. Masson (Frankfurt am Main, 1986), here 293 (letter of October 15, 1897). For the English translation, see *The Complete Letters of Sigmund Freud to Wilhelm Fliess, 1887–1904*, trans. J. M. Masson (Cambridge, Mass., 1985), 270–273.

15. Stephan discusses the problem of the identification of Anna with Antigone, "Im Zeichen der Sphinx," 18; cf. also O. H. Blomfield, "Anna Freud: Creativity, Compassion, Discipline," *International Review of Psycho-Analysis* 18.1 (1991), 37–52.

16. See Vogt, *Psychoanalyse zwischen Mythos und Aufklärung*, 103–154.

17. Freud's antiquities collection is almost entirely located in the house at 20 Maresfield Gardens in Hampstead where Freud lived the last year of his life (now the London Freud Museum). See the important catalogue edited by L. Gamwell and R. Wells, *Sigmund Freud and Art: His Personal Collection of Antiquities* (London,

1989). It was produced for the exhibition *The Sigmund Freud Antiquities: Fragments from a Buried Past,* which opened in Philadelphia in 1989 and inspired further exhibitions and publications, such as E. Gubel, ed., *Le sphinx de Vienne: Sigmund Freud, l'art et l'archéologie* (Ghent, 1993); S. Barker, ed., *Excavations and Their Objects: Freud's Collection of Antiquities* (Albany, NY, 1996); and L. Marinelli, ed., *"Meine . . . alten und dreckigen Götter": Aus Sigmund Freuds Sammlung* (Frankfurt am Main, 1998).

18. Cf. J. Burke, *The Sphinx on the Table: Sigmund Freud's Art Collection and the Development of Psychoanalysis* (New York, 2006).

19. Freud cites these lines in *The Interpretation of Dreams,* 203.

20. On the significance and history of the press see the catalog essays from the 1995 exhibition on the International Psychoanalytic Press (Sigmund Freud Museum, Vienna, 1995); on the logo, see Sigmund Freud Museum, Vienna, *Internationaler Psychoanalytischer Verlag 1919–1938* (Sigmund Freud House Bulletins), Special issue 1 (1995), 8.

21. Figures of the bookplate and two versions of the logo are to be found in R. H. Armstrong, *A Compulsion for Antiquity: Freud and the Ancient World* (Ithaca, 2005), 54–55.

22. Armstrong, *A Compulsion for Antiquity,* 52–55.

23. E. Jones, *Sigmund Freud, Life and Work,* (London, 1955), vol. 2, 15. On the anecdote as a psychoanalytical parable, see P. L. Rudnytsky, *Freud and Oedipus* (New York, 1987), 4–6.

24. On the analogy of the riddle solver, see also Armstrong, *A Compulsion for Antiquity,* 52–56.

25. C. Rohde-Dachser, *Expedition in den dunklen Kontinent: Weiblichkeit im Diskurs der Psychoanalyse* (Berlin, 1991).

26. See also Vogt, *Psychoanalyse zwischen Mythos und Aufklärung,* 152f.

27. See also Rohde-Dachser, *Expedition in den dunklen Kontinent.*

28. For her English translation, Joyce Crick has selected F. E. Watling's translation of *Oedipus the King* (Harmondsworth, 1964). Line 1525 of *Oedipus the King* reads: ὃς τὰ κλείν' αἰνίγματ' ᾔδει καὶ κράτιστος ἦν ἀνήρ. A more precise rendering would be: "he who unraveled the great riddle, and was a most powerful man."

29. Freud, *The Interpretation of Dreams,* 203 (*GW* 2/3: 269).

30. Freud quoted from the edition, very popular at the time, *Sophokles, deutsch in den Versmaßen der Urschrift v. J. J. C. Donner,* first published in 1839 (by Winter in Leipzig), and reprinted and revised for a seventh edition in 1873, the year of Freud's school-leaving examination, for which he was, as his youthful letters to Emil Fluß testify (letter of March 17, 1873), examined on *OT.* Donner translates the final chorus as follows: "Ihr Bewohner meines Thebens, sehet, das ist Oidipus, / Der entwirrt die hohen Rätsel und der Erste war an Macht, / Dessen Glück die Bürger alle priesen und beneideten, / Seht, in welches Missgeschickes grause Wogen er versank! / Drum der Erdensöhne keinen, welcher noch auf jenen Tag / Harrt, den letzten seiner Tage, preise du vorher beglückt, / Eh er drang ans Ziel des Lebens, unberührt von Schmerz und Leid."

31. Soph. *OT* 132.

32. Freud, *The Interpretation of Dreams,* 201 (*GW* 2/3: 267).

33. Freud, *The Interpretation of Dreams,* 203 (*GW* 2/3: 270).

34. Freud, "A Difficulty in the Path of Psycho-Analysis" (1917), *SE* 17: 135–144, here 143 ("Eine Schwierigkeit der Psychoanalyse" [*GW* 12: 3–12, here 11]).

Chapter Four

1. On Freud's use of the term *Deutungskunst* ("art of interpretation"), cf. M. Bartels, *Selbstbewusstsein und Unbewusstes: Studien zu Freud und Heidegger* (Berlin, 1976), 34–38.

2. "La clef de songes de Freud est forte naïve. Le simple s'y baptise complexe. Son obsession sexuelle devait séduire une société oisive dont le sexe est l'axe." J. Cocteau, *Journal d'un inconnu* (Grasse 1952), 40. Freud's *Traumdeutung* appeared in French in 1926 under the title *La science des rêves*, and recurs frequently in Cocteau as "clef de songes," e.g. in *Journal d'un inconnu*, 158; *Le Testament d'Orphée* (Monaco, 1961), 69; and *Le Cordon Ombilical: Souvenirs* (Paris, 1962), 49.

3. "Freud a raison de dire, [. . .] qu'un artiste n'a pas besoin d' avoir pensé à certaines choses pour que ces choses deviennent ensuite le principal objet de son œuvre." J. Cocteau, "Le sang d'un poète," in Cocteau, *Du cinématographe: Textes réunis et présentés par André Bernard et Claude Gauteur* (Paris, 1973), 103f., here 104.

4. "En effet, ce que nous mettons dans un film de nos ombres, de nos ténèbres, notre poésie en quelque sorte, ne nous regarde pas et ne doit être décelé que par ceux qui nous jugent." J. Cocteau, "Poésie et films," in *Du cinématographe*, 26–28, here 26.

5. Cocteau uses adjectives like "naïf", "mediocre", "pauvre", and "assez vulgaire." Cf. K. Rave, *Orpheus bei Cocteau: Psychoanalytische Studie zu Jean Cocteaus dichterischem Selbstverständnis* (Frankfurt am Main, 1984), 12–15.

6. Cf. Rave, *Orpheus bei Cocteau*, esp. 12–15.

7. On Cocteau's understanding of dream (in contrast to those of the Surrealists and Freud), see H. R. Kautz, *Dichtung und Kunst in der Theorie Jean Cocteaus* (Diss., Heidelberg, 1970), esp. 133–146 and 190–197; S. Winter, *Jean Cocteaus frühe Lyrik: Poetische Praxis und poetologische Reflexion* (Berlin, 1994), 137–141; and V. Borsò, "Der Orpheus-Mythos neu geträumt: Anmerkungen zu Jean Cocteaus Theater und Film," in *Antike Dramen neu gelesen, neu gesehen: Beiträge zur Antikenrezeption in der Gegenwart*, ed. K. Hölz et al. (Frankfurt am Main, 1998), 77–97, here 88–90.

8. "Le démon de comprendre. C'est sans doute le péché originel du paradis de l'art." J. Cocteau, *Démarche d'un Poète: Der Lebensweg eines Dichters* (Munich, 1953), 25.

9. "La manie de comprendre—alors que le monde que les gens habitent et les actes de Dieu sont en apparence incohérents, contradictoires et incompréhensibles—la manie de comprendre, dis-je, les ferme à toutes les grandes vagues exquises que l'art déroule aux solitudes où l'homme ne cherche plus à comprendre mais à ressentir." J. Cocteau, "La poésie au cinématographe," in *Du cinématographe*, 31.

10. N. Bolz, *Eine kurze Geschichte des Scheins* (Munich, 1991), 31: "ikonoklastischen Grundzug der Psychoanalyse."

11. T. W. Adorno, *Minima Moralia* (1951: Frankfurt am Main, 1970), 298: "Aufgabe von Kunst ist es heute, Chaos in die Ordnung zu bringen."

12. Freud, *Interpretation of Dreams*, 402 (*GW* 2/3: 613).

13. Freud, *Interpretation of Dreams*, 247 (*GW* 2/3: 329).

14. J. Cocteau, *Opium*, in Cocteau, *Romans, poésies, poésie critique, théâtre, cinéma* (Paris, 1995), 667.

15. See, e.g., the chapter "Reception," in A. B. Evans, *Jean Cocteau and His Films of Orphic Identity* (Philadelphia, 1969), 53–65.

16. J. Cocteau, *Le Cordon Ombilical: Souvenirs* (Paris, 1962), 19.

17. Other terms used are *moi inconnu* and *moi secret*; references in Kautz, *Dichtung und Kunst in der Theorie Jean Cocteaus*, 138.

18. "Un poète se doit d'accepter ce que sa nuit lui dicte comme un dormeur accepte le rêve." J. Cocteau, *Notes sur le Testament d'Orphée* (Liège, 1960), 6.

19. Cocteau, *Journal d'un inconnu*, 19: "Ce doit être ce fil au-dessus du vide qui nous fait traiter d'acrobates, et le passage de nos secrets à la lumière, véritable travail d'archéologue, qui nous fait prendre pour des prestidigateurs."

20. Cocteau, Preface to *Le Testament d'Orphée*, 1322. Traveling in the Middle East in 1949, Cocteau was already drawing parallels in his diary (*Maalesh: Journal d'une tournée de théâtre* [Paris, 1949], 104) between his work and that of an archaeologist: "Depuis trente ans, je me fouille et je me déchiffre. Lorsque Varille [un archéologue] me commente un temple, je crois l'entendre m'expliquer le mécanisme de *La machine infernale*. . ." See also Cocteau, *Romans, poésies, poésie critique, théâtre, cinéma*, 1116.

21. See, e.g., D. Kuspit, "A Mighty Metaphor: The Analogy of Archaeology and Psychoanalysis," in *Sigmund Freud and Art: His Personal Collection of Antiquities*, ed. L. Gamwell and R. Wells (London, 1989), 133–151; K. Reinhard, "The Freudian Things: Construction and the Archaeological Metaphor," in *Excavations and Their Objects: Freud's Collection of Antiquity*, ed. S. Barker (Albany, 1996), 57–79; W. Mertens and R. Haubl, *Der Psychoanalytiker als Archäologe* (Stuttgart, 1996); K. Stockreiter, "Am Rand der Aufklärungsmetapher: Korrespondenzen zwischen Archäologie und Psychoanalyse," in *"Meine . . . alten und dreckigen Götter": Aus Sigmund Freuds Sammlung*, ed. L. Marinelli (Vienna, 1998), 81–93; R. H. Armstrong, *A Compulsion for Antiquity*; G. Pollock, "The Image in Psychoanalysis and the Archaeological Metaphor," in Pollock, *Psychoanalysis and the Image: Transdisciplinary Perspectives* (Malden, Mass., 2006), 1–29.

22. S. Freud, *The Future of an Illusion* (1927), *SE* 21: 5–57, here 54f. (*Die Zukunft einer Illusion*, *GW* 14: 325–380, here 378).

23. Cocteau, *Journal d'un inconnu*, 142.

24. E.g., already in *Studies on Hysteria* (1895), *SE* 2: 1–252, here 139f. (*Studien über Hysterie GW* 1: 77–312, here 201).

25. On this matter, see, e.g., R. Ransohoff, "Sigmund Freud: Collector of Antiquities, Student of Archaeology," *Archaeology* 28 (1975), 102–111; C. Weiß and H. Weiß, "Dem Beispiel jener Forscher folgend . . . Zur Bedeutung der Archäologie im Leben Freuds," *Luzifer-Amor: Zeitschrift zur Geschichte der Psychoanalyse* 3 (1989), 45–71; and J. Burke, *The Gods of Freud: Sigmund Freud's Art Collection* (Milsons Point, New South Wales, 2006).

26. S. Freud, "Der Wahn und die Träume in W. Jensens 'Gradiva'" (1907), in *GW* 7: 31–125; passages concerned with archaeology: 64f.; 76–79; 112f.; 116–119 (*SE* 9: 7–93). On Cocteau's presumable knowledge of the treatise, see Rave, *Orpheus bei Cocteau*, 8. Jensen's protagonist, Norbert Hanold, an unworldly archaeologist, goes to Pompeii in search of a relief figure after dreaming of seeing the figure come to life. At Pompeii, he ultimately recognizes the image as a lover from his youth back

home. Freud read Jensen's 1903 novella strictly in terms of dream interpretation, to explain the mechanisms of the unconscious. In the process, he assumed that the protagonist symbolically represented aspects of the poet Wilhelm Jensen, so that the excavation of an earlier cultural phase, such as appears fragmented but preserved at Pompeii, became a metaphor for the unearthing and reconstruction of childhood propensities in an individual's life.

27. Cocteau, *Démarche d'un Poète*, 10 and 25.

28. "C'est de notre réserve, de notre nuit, que les choses nous viennent. Notre oeuvre préexiste en nous. Le problème consiste à la *découvrir* (invenire). Nous n'en sommes que les archéologues." J. Cocteau, *Entretiens autour du cinématographe*, ed. André Fraigneau (Paris, 1951), 159.

29. The use of the term "plus vrai que le vrai" to characterize a transcendental truth behind the visible world that the poet is capable of revealing is found in many places throughout Cocteau's work, e.g., in *Opium, Orphée* (film), *Le Testament d'Orphée*, but also — already — in the early 1920s, e.g., in an impression of Picasso, from whom Cocteau learned that the artist's scope for expression is infinite, and of whom, deeply impressed, he said that he could enchant objects like Orpheus; *Picasso* (1923): in *Le Rappel à l'ordre* (Paris, 1926), 287.

30. Cocteau, *Journal d'un inconnu*, 18.

31. See also the "Nachwort," in J. Cocteau, *Werkausgabe in zwölf Bänden*, ed. Reinhard Schmidt, vol. 4, *Theater I* (Frankfurt am Main, 1988), 316f.

32. There are many studies on the subject of Freud and religion, written from highly varying perspectices (pro and contra Freud), e.g., H. Racker, "On Freud's Position Towards Religion," *American Imago* 13 (1956): 97–121; H. Philp, *Freud and Religious Belief* (London, 1956); P. Homans, *Theology after Freud* (Indianapolis, 1970); R. Rainey, *Freud as Student of Religion: Perspectives on the Background and Development of his Thought* (Missoula, 1975); H. Küng, *Freud and the Problem of God* (New Haven, 1979); Peter Gay, *A Godless Jew: Freud, Atheism, and the Making of Psychoanalysis* (New Haven, 1987); J. Scharfenberg, *Sigmund Freud and His Critique of Religion* (Philadelphia, 1988); and S. Handelman and J. Smith, eds., *Psychoanalysis and Religion* (Baltimore, 1990).

33. Cocteau, *Journal d'un inconnu*, 40.

34. Ibid., 42.

35. Ibid., 39.

36. Ibid.; see also D. Marny, *Die Schönen Cocteaus: Biographie* (Hamburg, 1999), 9f.

37. See, e.g., Milorad, "La Clé des mythes dans l'œuvre de Cocteau," *Cahiers Jean Cocteau* 2 (1971): 97–140; K. Rave, *Orpheus bei Cocteau* ; and G. Albrechtskirchinger, "Klassische Mythen im Werk Jean Cocteau," in J. Poetter (ed.), *J. Cocteau: Gemälde, Zeichnungen, Keramik, Tapisserien, Literatur, Theater, Film, Ballett*, Exhibition Catalogue (Cologne, 1989), 310–321.

38. Rave, *Orpheus bei Cocteau*, 111–122, postulates three fundamental types to which most of these female figures can be ascribed: (1) the acquiescent, submissive type who looks up to her son and is always there for him; (2) the lofty and masterful type who looks down on her son; (3) a hybrid type, a mixture of types 1 and 2.

39. Freud, *Interpretation of Dreams*, 202 (*GW* 2/3: 269).

40. E.g. H. R. Kautz, *Dichtung und Kunst in der Theorie Jean Cocteaus*.

41. Cocteau emphasizes this above all in 1930 in *Opium* (following the insight that, contrary to the hopes he still entertained in the 1920s, he could not attain the "invisible" and become its poetic master through opium, but he could only draw near to it).

42. J. Cocteau, *Clair-obscur: Poèmes* (Monaco, 1954), 47f.

43. J. Cocteau, *Le testament d'Orphée* (Liège, 1960), 38.

44. "La Zone est 'faite du souvenir des humains et de la ruine de leurs habitudes.' Elle n'empiète sur aucun dogme. Elle est un no man's land entre la vie et la mort. La seconde du coma, en quelque sorte." Cocteau, *Entretiens autour du cinématographe*, 154.

45. Vittoria Borsò has demonstrated this procedure using the example of the film and theater play *Orphée*: Borsò, "Der Orpheus-Mythos neu geträumt."

46. Barthes wrote a number of texts between 1954 and 1956 examining modern myths (in areas as diverse as film, television, cooking, and photography), their origins, and a tendency of value systems to create modern myths. Barthes revised the sign system of analysis (semiotics) first suggested by Ferdinand de Saussure, and added another level which elevates signs to a mythic rank. The texts appeared in 1957 for the first time as a collection under the title *Mythologies* in Paris; for an English translation see: R. Barthes, *Mythologies*, trans. A. Lavers (London, 1972).

47. On the topic, see, e.g., E. Bronfen and B. Straumann, *Diva: Geschichte einer Bewunderung* (Munich, 2002).

48. As evidenced by film and documentary biographies, such as M. Schell, *Marlene Dietrich: Portrait eines Mythos* (Munich: Bayerischer Rundfunk, 1983), VHS, 94 min.; J. Vilsmaier, *Marlene: Die Legende, der Mythos, der Film* (Manaus: Imagem Filmes 2000), DVD, 126 min.; M. Unterburg, *Mythos Marlene: Die Dietrich und das 'Dritte Reich'* (Mainz: ZDF, 2004), VHS, 43 min. See also *Mythos Marlene Dietrich*, ed. C. Auderlitzky et al. (catalogue for the exhibition *Mythos Marlene Dietrich*, 6 May–5 November 2007, Österreichische Filmgalerie) (Krems, 2007).

49. "Marlène Dietrich . . . , Votre nom débute par une caresse et finit par un coup de cravache. Vous portez des plumes et des fourrures, qui semblent appartenir à votre corps comme les fourrures des fauves et les plumes des oiseaux." Cocteau, "Marlene Dietrich," in *Du cinématographe*, 60.

50. "Mais Lorelei était dangereuse; vous ne l'êtes pas parce que votre secret de beauté consiste à prendre soin de votre ligne de cœur. C'est votre ligne de cœur qui vous place au-dessus de l'élégance, au-dessus des modes, au-dessus des styles: au-dessus même de votre courage, de votre démarche, de vos films et des vos chansons." Ibid.

51. Cocteau, "Charlie Chaplin" and "James Dean," in *Du cinématographe*, 57–59.

52. "Un des signes de notre époque est de créer des mythes immédiats dans tous les domaines. La presse se charge d'inventer certains personnages qui existent et de les affubler d'une vie imaginaire superposée à la leur. Brigitte Bardot nous offre un exemple parfait de cet étrange mélange. Il est probable que le destin l'a mise à la place exacte où le rêve et la réalité se confondent. Sa beauté, son talent sont incontestables, mais elle possède autre chose d'inconnu qui attire les idolâtres d'un âge privé de dieux." Cocteau, "Brigitte Bardot," in *Du cinématographe*, 55.

53. Cf. A. B. Evans, *Jean Cocteau and His Films of Orphic Identity* (Philadelphia, 1969), 66–83.

54. Cocteau in the aforementioned interview with André Fraigneau, in reply to the question of why he produced stage plays, drawings, and films. *Entretiens autour du cinématographe*, 157.

55. J. Cocteau, "Orphée," in *Du cinématographe*, 124–130, here 128.

56. "Je suis un poète qui use de la caméra comme d'un véhicule propre à permettre à tous de rêver ensemble un même rêve, un rêve qui n'est pas un rêve de sommeil mais le rêve rêvé debout, qui n'est autre que le réalisme irréel, le plus vrai que le vrai." Cocteau, letter to Régis Bastide (= *Les lettres françaises*, 11 February 1960), in Cocteau, *Du cinématographe*, 144–146, here 146.

57. Cocteau, *Opium*, 678. Both figures also constantly interested him as a pictorial artist. Visual depictions of both the Sphinx and Oedipus figures are found scattered throughout his work; e.g., J. Poetter, ed., *J. Cocteau: Gemälde, Zeichnungen, Keramik, Tapisserien, Literatur, Theater, Film, Ballett* (Cologne, 1989), 314f. (nos. 254, 88: Œdipe), and 380f. (nos. 500, 511, 512: Sphinx).

58. On the terminology, see above the "introduction," especially footnote 6.

59. Cocteau scholars seldom discuss the Seneca reference, but focus on the Shakespearean element in the apparition of the ghost (comparison with Hamlet's father). See, e.g., P. G. Mason, "*La machine infernale*: A Modern Adaptation of the Oedipus Legend by Jean Cocteau," *Greece & Rome* 9.27 (1940), 178–187, here 180f.; A. Belli, *Ancient Greek Myths and Modern Drama* (New York, 1969), 5–19, here 17f.; K. V. Hartigan, "Oedipus in France: Cocteau's Mythic Strategy in *La machine infernale*," *Classical and Modern Literature* 6.2 (1986), 89–95, here 90; and R. Guerini, "*La macchina infernale* di Jean Cocteau," *Studi di letteratura francese* 15 (1989): 140–167.

60. Sen. *Oed.* 388–393.

61. J. Cocteau, *La machine infernale: Pièce en quatre actes*, ed. Paul Ginestier (Paris, 1961), 26.

62. For a comprehensive account, see W. Frick, *"Die mythische Methode": Komparatistische Studien zur Transformation der griechischen Tragödie im Drama der Klassischen Moderne* (Tübingen, 1998), 388–396.

63. Antigone's decision to accompany her blind father goes back to Sophocles' *Oedipus Coloneus*, where, after years of exile, the aged Oedipus appears, accompanied by his daughter Antigone, at the hill of Colonus in Athens, where the sacred grove of the Erinyes is found, to plead for release from his life of suffering.

64. *Machine infernale*, 136.

65. Ibid., 134.

66. Cocteau, *Opium*, 678. See also "Nachwort," in Cocteau, *Werkausgabe in zwölf Bänden*, 4:318.

67. *Machine infernale*, 61f.

68. Ibid., 73.

69. Cocteau, *Entretiens autour du cinématographe*, 154.

70. On the concept and codified aesthetic of the ruin, see H. Böhme, "Die Ästhetik der Ruinen," in *Der Schein des Schönen*, ed. D. Kamper and C. Wulf (Göttingen, 1989), 287–304.

71. Luc. *Dial. Mar.* 7.2.

72. H. Bonnet, "Anubis," in *Reallexikon der ägyptischen Religionsgeschichte* (Berlin, 1952), 40–45.

73. Soph. *OT* 391; *Machine infernale*, 80.

74. *Machine infernale*, 62.

75. Ibid., 87.

76. Hes. *Theog.* 211f., 223f.

77. Eur. *Phoen.* 182–184; Pl. *Leg.* 717d; Catull. 68, 77–80.

78. Cocteau, *Journal d'un inconnu*, 41.

79. Bonnet, "Anubis," 44. Examples of Hermes as psychopomp in Greek literature: Hom. *Od.* 11.626; 24.1ff.; Hom. *Hymn Dem.* 2.335ff.

80. *Machine infernale*, 63.

81. Cocteau, *Le Testament d'Orphée*, 38.

82. E.g., W. Hofmann, "Evas neue Kleider," in *Eva und die Zukunft: Das Bild der Frau seit der Französischen Revolution*, ed. Hofmann (Munich, 1986), 13: "The image of woman is man's image of woman. [. . .] In the images man makes of the other sex, he is himself inherent. In the Other, he evokes the wishful image that he invents for himself of his own role in the dialogue of the genders."

83. "[. . .] plus adroit qu'un aveugle, plus rapide que le filet des gladiateurs, plus subtil que la foudre, plus raide qu'un cocher, plus lourd qu'une vache, plus sage qu'un élève tirant la langue sur des chiffres, plus gréé, plus voilé, plus ancré, plus bercé qu'un navire, plus incorruptible qu'un juge, plus vorace que les insectes, plus sanguinaire que les oiseaux, plus nocturne que l'œuf, plus ingénieux que les bourreaux d'Asie, plus fourbe que le cœur, plus désinvolte qu'une main qui triche, plus fatal que les astres, plus attentif que le serpent qui humecte sa proie de salive; je sécrète, je tire de moi, je lâche, je dévide, je déroule, j'enroule de telle sorte qu'il me suffira de vouloir ces nœuds pour les faire et d'y penser pour les tendre ou pour les détendre; si mince qu'il t'échappe, si souple que tu t'imagineras être victime de quelque poison, [. . .] machiné comme les décors du rêve, invisible surtout, invisible et majestueux." *Machine infernale*, 82f.

84. "Et je parle, je travaille, je dévide, je déroule, je calcule, je médite, je tresse, je vanne, je tricote, je natte, je croise, je passe, je repasse, je noue et dénoue et renoue, [. . .] j'enchevêtre, désenchevêtre, délace, entrelace, repars; et j'ajuste, j'agglutine, je garrotte, je sangle, j'entrave, j'accumule, jusqu'à ce que tu te sentes, de la pointe des pieds à la racine des cheveux, vêtu de toutes les boucles d'un seul reptile dont la moindre respiration coupe la tienne." Ibid., 83.

85. Ibid.

86. "Je veux bien que le public français soit impropre à l'hypnose collective, lui résiste de toutes les forces de son individualisme et veuille prouver son intelligence par la critique." Cocteau, "La poésie au cinématographe," in *Du cinématographe*, 28–31, here 30.

87. Cocteau, *Journal d'un inconnu*, 41.

BIBLIOGRAPHY

ঞ

Abbreviations

DNP   *Der neue Pauly: Enzyklopädie der Antike*, ed. Cancik, H., and Schneider, H.,
       16 vols. Stuttgart, 1996–2003.
FGrH   *Die Fragmente der griechischen Historiker*, ed. F. Jacoby, 3 vols. Leiden, 1954–
       1964.
GW   Freud, S., *Gesammelte Werke*, ed. A. Freud et al., with the participation of
       Marie Bonaparte, 17 vols. London, 1940.
LIMC   *Lexicon iconographicum mythologiae classicae*, 8 vols., plus Supplement,
       2 vols. Zürich, 1981–2009.
OT   Sophocles, *Oedipus Tyrannus*, in *Sophoclis Fabulae*, ed. H. Lloyd-Jones.
       Oxford, 1990.
RE   *Paulys Realencyclopädie der classischen Altertumswissenschaft*, ed. G. Wissowa,
       49 vols. Stuttgart, 1894–1980.
SE   Freud, S., *The Standard Edition of the Complete Psychological Works of
       Sigmund Freud*, 24 vols., ed. James Strachey. London, 1953–1974.

Works Cited

Adorno, T. W., *Minima Moralia* (1951). Frankfurt am Main, 1970.
Albrechtskirchinger, G., "Klassische Mythen im Werk Jean Cocteau," in J. Poetter,
       ed., *J. Cocteau* (1989), 310–321.
Andrus, T. W., "Oedipus Revisited: Cocteau's 'Poésie de théâtre,'" *French Review* 48
       (1975), 722–728.
Armstrong, R. H., *A Compulsion for Antiquity: Freud and the Ancient World*. Ithaca,
       2005.

Astier, C., *Le mythe d'Oedipe*. Paris, 1974.

Auderlitzky, C., et al., eds., *Mythos Marlene Dietrich*. Catalogue for the exhibition *Mythos Marlene Dietrich*, 6 May–5 November 2007, Österreichische Filmgalerie. Krems, 2007.

Barker, S., ed., *Excavations and Their Objects: Freud's Collection of Antiquities*. Albany, 1996.

Bartels, M., *Selbstbewusstsein und Unbewusstes: Studien zu Freud und Heidegger*. Berlin, 1976.

Barthes, R., *Mythologies*, trans. A. Lavers. London, 1972.

Bauschatz, P., "Œdipus: Stravinsky and Cocteau Recompose Sophocles," *Comparative Literature* 43 (1991), 150–170.

Belli, A., *Ancient Greek Myths and Modern Drama*. New York, 1969.

Benjamin, W., *Das Passagen-Werk*, 2 vols., ed. R. Tiedemann. Frankfurt am Main, 1983. [*The Arcades Project*, trans. H. Eiland and K. McLaughlin. Cambridge, MA, 1999]

Bernabé, A., ed., *Poetae epici Graeci: Testimonia et fragmenta*, vol. 1, Leipzig, 1987 (= *PEG I*).

Bierl, A., "Religion und Literatur," *DNP* 15.2 (2002), col. 669–677.

——, "Literatur und Religion als Rito- und Mythopoetik: Überblicksartikel zu einem neuen Ansatz in der Klassischen Philologie," in *Literatur und Religion 1: Wege zu einer mythisch-rituellen Poetik bei den Griechen*, ed. A. Bierl, R. Lämmle and K. Wesselmann. Berlin, 2007, 1–76.

Blomfield, O. H., "Anna Freud: Creativity, Compassion, Discipline," *International Review of Psycho-Analysis* 18.1 (1991), 37–52.

Boardman, J., *The History of Greek Vases: Potters, Painters and Pictures*. London, 2001.

Böhme, H., "Die Ästhetik der Ruinen," in *Der Schein des Schönen*, ed. D. Kamper and C. Wulf. Göttingen, 1989, 287–304.

Bollack, J., *L'Oedipe roi de Sophocle: Le texte et ses interprétations*, 4 vols. Lille, 1990.

Bolz, N., *Eine kurze Geschichte des Scheins*. Munich, 1991.

Bonnet, H., "Anubis," in *Reallexikon der ägyptischen Religionsgeschichte*. Berlin, 1952, 40–45.

Boorsch, J., "The Use of Myths in Cocteau's Theatre," *Yale French Studies* 5 (1950), 75–81.

Borsò, V., "Der Orpheus-Mythos neu geträumt: Anmerkungen zu Jean Cocteaus Theater und Film," in *Antike Dramen neu gelesen, neu gesehen: Beiträge zur Antikenrezeption in der Gegenwart*, ed. K. Hölz et al. Frankfurt am Main, 1998, 77–97.

Brach, W., *Der Œdipe von Corneille und der des Voltaire, verglichen mit dem Oedipus Rex des Sophokles* (Doct. Diss.), Marburg an der Lahn, 1914.

Bremmer, J., "Oedipus and the Greek Oedipus Complex," in *Interpretations of Greek Mythology*, ed. J. Bremmer. London, 1987, 41–59.

Brittnacher, H. R., *Ästhetik des Horrors: Gespenster, Vampire, Monster, Teufel und künstliche Menschen in der phantastischen Literatur*. Frankfurt am Main, 1994.

Bronfen, E., and Straumann, B., *Diva: Geschichte einer Bewunderung*. Munich, 2002.

Brosi, S., *Der Kuß der Sphinx: Weibliche Gestalten nach griechischem Mythos in Malerei und Graphik des Symbolismus*. Münster, 1993.

Burke, J., *The Gods of Freud: Sigmund Freud's Art Collection*. Milsons Point, New South Wales, 2006.

————, *The Sphinx on the Table: Sigmund Freud's Art Collection and the Development of Psychoanalysis*. New York, 2006.

Calame, C., "Le nom d'Œdipe," in *Edipo: Il teatro greco e la cultura europea*, ed. B. Gentili and R. Pretagostini. Rome, 1986, 395–407.

Cocteau, J., *Le Rappel à l'ordre*. Paris, 1926.

————, *Maalesh: Journal d'une tournée de théâtre*. Paris, 1949.

————, *Entretiens autour du cinématographe*, ed. André Fraigneau. Paris, 1951.

————, *Journal d'un inconnu*. Grasse, 1952.

————, *Démarche d'un Poète: Der Lebensweg eines Dichters*. Munich, 1953.

————, *Clair-obscur: Poèmes*. Monaco, 1954.

————, *Notes sur le Testament d'Orphée*. Liège, 1960.

————, *La machine infernale: Pièce en quatre actes*, ed. Paul Ginestier. Paris, 1961.

————, *Le Testament d'Orphée*. Monaco, 1961.

————, *Le Cordon Ombilical: Souvenirs*. Paris, 1962.

————, *Du cinématographe: Textes réunis et présentés par André Bernard et Claude Gauteur*. Paris, 1973.

————, *Werkausgabe in zwölf Bänden*, vol. 4, *Theater I*, ed. Reinhard Schmidt. Frankfurt am Main, 1988.

————, *Romans, poésies, poésie critique, théâtre, cinéma*. Paris, 1995.

Corneille, *Œuvres complètes* (Bibliothèque de la Pléiade): *Textes établis, présentés et annotés*, 3 vols., ed. G. Couton. Paris, 1987.

Crowson, L., *The Esthetic of Jean Cocteau*. Hanover, New Hampshire, 1978.

Daly, L. W., "Oedipus," *RE* 17, col. 2103–2117 and *RE* Suppl. 7, col. 769–786.

Daskarolis, A. *Die Wiedergeburt des Sophokles aus dem Geist des Humanismus: Studien zur Sophokles-Rezeption in Deutschland vom Beginn des 16. bis Mitte des 17. Jahrhunderts*. Tübingen, 2000.

Dawe, R. D., ed., *Sophocles: The Classical Heritage*. New York, 1996.

————, "On Interpolations in the Two Oedipus Plays of Sophocles," *Rheinisches Museum für Philologie* 144 (2001), 1–21.

de Beauvoir, S., *The Second Sex* (1949). New York, 1989.

de Kock, E. L., "The Sophoklean Oidipus and Its Antecedents," *Acta classica* 4 (1961), 7–28.

Delcourt, M., *Légendes et cultes de héros en Grèce*. Paris, 1942.

————, ed., *Œdipe ou la légende du conquérant* (1944). Paris, 1981.

Demisch, H., *Die Sphinx: Geschichte ihrer Darstellung von den Anfängen bis zur Gegenwart*. Stuttgart, 1977.

Deubner, L., *Oedipusprobleme*. Berlin, 1942.

di Benedetto, V., *Sofocle*. Florence, 1983.

Dijkstra, B., *Idols of Perversity: Fantasies of Feminine Evil in Fin-de-Siècle Culture*. New York, 1986.

Dubiel, U., "Pharao—Gott—Wächter: Sphingen im Alten Ägypten," in Winkler-Horáček, *Wege der Sphinx* (2011), 5–25.

Dumarty, H., "Le mythe dans l'oeuvre de Cocteau: La rencontre d'un signe et d'une intention," *Revue de l'Université de Bruxelles* 1–2 (1989), 23–40.

Edmunds, L., *The Sphinx in the Oedipus Legend* (*Beiträge zur klassischen Philologie* 127). Königstein, Ts., 1981.

————, *Oedipus: The Ancient Legend and Its Later Analogues.* Baltimore, 1985.

Eschenburg, B., and Friedel, H., eds., *Der Kampf der Geschlechter: Der neue Mythos in der Kunst 1850–1930.* Exhibition Catalogue. Munich, 1995.

Evans, A. B., *Jean Cocteau and His Films of Orphic Identity.* Philadelphia, 1969.

Febel, G., "Mythen-Bricolage in Film und Theater Frankreichs—das Beispiel Jean Cocteau," in *Mythenkorrekturen: Zu einer paradoxalen Form der Mythenrezeption,* ed. M. Vöhler and B. Seidensticker. Berlin, 2005, 331–343.

Flaake, K., "Psychoanalyse," in *Gender-Studien: eine Einführung,* ed. C. von Braun and I. Stephan. Stuttgart, 2000, 169–179.

Flaig, E., *Ödipus: Tragischer Vatermord im klassischen Athen.* Munich, 1998.

Flashar, H., "König Ödipus: Drama und Theorie," *Gymnasium* 84 (1977), 120–136 (reprinted in *Eidola: Ausgewählte Kleine Schriften* [Amsterdam, 1989], 57–73).

————, "Die Poetik des Aristoteles und die griechische Tragödie," *Poetica* 16 (1984), 1–23.

————, *Sophokles: Dichter im demokratischen Athen.* Munich, 2000.

Foucault, M., "Introduction," in *Traum und Existenz,* ed. Binswanger. Bern/Berlin, 1992, 7–93.

Freud, S., *Briefe an Wilhelm Fliess 1887–1904: Ungekürzte Ausgabe,* ed. J. M. Masson. Frankfurt am Main, 1986 [*The Complete Letters of Sigmund Freud to Wilhelm Fliess, 1887–1904,* trans. J. M. Masson. Cambridge, MA, 1985].

————, *The Interpretation of Dreams,* trans. J. Crick. Oxford, 1999.

Frick, W., *'Die mythische Methode': Komparatistische Studien zur Transformation der griechischen Tragödie im Drama der klassischen Moderne.* Tübingen, 1998.

Friedrich, W. H., "Ein Ödipus mit gutem Gewissen: Über Corneilles Oedipe," in *Vorbild und Neugestaltung: Sechs Kapitel zur Geschichte der Tragödie,* ed. Friedrich. Göttingen, 1967, 112–139.

Gamwell, L., and Wells, R., *Sigmund Freud and Art: His Personal Collection of Antiquities.* London, 1989.

Gantz, T., *Early Greek Myth: A Guide to Literary and Artistic Sources.* Baltimore, 1993.

Gay, P., *A Godless Jew: Freud, Atheism, and the Making of Psychoanalysis.* New Haven, 1987.

Genette, G., *Palimpsestes: La littérature au second degré.* Paris, 1982 [*Palimpsests: Literature in the Second Degree,* trans. C. Newman and C. Doubinsky. Lincoln, 1997].

Gernet, L., and Boilanger, A., *Le génie grec dans la religion.* Paris, 1932.

Gould, T., "The Innocence of Oedipus: The Philosophers on Oedipus the King," *Arion* 4 (1965), 363–386, 582–611; and *Arion* 5 (1966), 478–525.

Grosskurth, P., *Melanie Klein: Her World and Her Work.* New York, 1986.

Gubel, E., ed., *Le sphinx de Vienne: Sigmund Freud, l'art et l'archéologie.* Ghent, 1993.

Guerini, R., "La macchina infernale di Jean Cocteau," *Studi di letteratura francese* 15 (1989), 140–167.

Halter, T., *König Oedipus: Von Sophokles zu Cocteau.* Stuttgart, 1998.

Hamburger, K., *Von Sophokles zu Sartre.* Stuttgart, 1962.

Handelman, S., and Smith, J., ed., *Psychoanalysis and Religion.* Baltimore, 1990.

Hartigan, K. V., "Oedipus in France: Cocteau's Mythic Strategy in *La machine infernale,*" *Classical and Modern Literature* 6.2 (1986), 89–95.

Hausmann, U., "Oidipus und die Sphinx," *Jahrbuch der staatlichen Kunstsammlungen in Baden-Württemberg* 9 (1972), 7–36.

Henrichs, A., "Oidipus," *DNP* 8 (2000), col. 1129–1132.

Hilmes, C., "Sehnsucht nach Erlösung: Bilder des Weiblichen um 1900," in *Ästhetische und religiöse Erfahrungen der Jahrhundertwenden*, ed. W. Braungart. Paderborn, 1998, 276–289.

Hitchcock, S. T., *Karen Horney: Pioneer of Feminine Psychology*. Philadelphia, 2005.

Hofmann, W., "Evas neue Kleider," in *Eva und die Zukunft: Das Bild der Frau seit der Französischen Revolution*, ed. Hofmann. Munich, 1986, 13–21.

Homans, P., *Theology after Freud*. Indianapolis, 1970.

Hühn, H., "Oidipus," in *Mythenrezeption—Die antike Mythologie in Literatur, Kunst und Musik von den Anfängen bis zur Gegenwart (DNP*, Suppl. 5), ed. M. Moog-Grünewald. Stuttgart, 2008, 888–911.

Iberg, J. "Sphinx," in *Ausführliches Lexikon der griechischen und römischen Mythologie*, 7 vols., ed. W. H. Roscher. Leipzig, 1884–1937, vol. 4, col. 1298–1409.

Ivanovic, C., "Schwellen(w)orte: Phantastik zwischen Affirmation und Subversion," in *Macht und Mythos*, ed. T. Le Blanc and B. Twrsnick. Wetzlar, 2005, 13–36.

Jones, E., *Sigmund Freud, Life and Work*, 2 vols. London, 1955.

Jördens, W., *Die französischen Ödipusdramen: Ein Beitrag zum Fortleben der Antike und zur Geschichte der französischen Tragödie*. Bochum, 1933.

Junker, K., *Interpreting the Images of Greek Myths: An Introduction*. Cambridge, 2012.

Kannicht, R., "Ein Hypomnema zum Ödipus des Euripides? P. Vindob. G 29779," *Würzburger Jahrbücher für die Altertumswissenschaft*, n.s. 1 (1975), 71–82.

Käppel, L., and Bäbler, B., "Perseus," *DNP* 9, col. 612–614.

Kautz, H. R., *Dichtung und Kunst in der Theorie Jean Cocteaus* (Doct. Diss.), Heidelberg, 1970.

Keuls, E. C., *Painter and Poet in Ancient Greece: Iconography and the Literary Arts*. Stuttgart, 1997.

Kimpel, H., and Werckmeister, J., "Die Schöne als das Biest: Zur Ikonographie der Sphinx," in *Don Juan und Femme fatale*, ed. H. H. Kreuzer. Munich, 1994, 117–125.

Knox, B., *Oedipus at Thebes*. New Haven, 1957.

———, "The Freedom of Oedipus," *New Republic* (Aug. 30, 1982), 28–34.

Kofler, W., and Korenjak, M., "Der literarische Ödipus: Ein Streifzug von der Antike bis Cocteau," in *Resonanzen: Innsbrucker Beiträge zum modernen Musiktheater bei den Salzburger Festspielen*, ed. C. Mühlegger and B. Schwarzmann-Huter. Innsbruck, 1998, 59–83.

Kourou, N., "Sphinx," *LIMC* 7.1.1152–1160.

Krauskopf, I., "Oidipous," *LIMC* 7.1.1–15.

Kristeva, J., *Melanie Klein* (European Perspectives: A Series in Social Thought and Cultural Criticism). New York, 2004.

Kühr, A., *Als Kadmos nach Boiotien kam: Polis und Ethnos im Spiegel thebanischer Gründungsmythen*. Stuttgart, 2006.

Kullmann, W., "Die Reaktionen auf die Orakel und ihre Erfüllung im *König Ödipus* des Sophokles," in *Orchestra: Drama, Mythos, Bühne* (Festschrift für H. Flashar), ed. A. Bierl and P. v. Möllendorff. Stuttgart, 1994, 105–118.

Küng, H., *Freud and the Problem of God*. New Haven, 1979.

Kuspit, D., "A Mighty Metaphor: The Analogy of Archaeology and Psychoanalysis," in Gamwell and Wells, *Sigmund Freud and Art*, (1989), 133–151.

Lascault, G., *Le monstre dans l'art occidentale: Un problème éthique*. Paris, 1973.

Latacz, J., *Einführung in die griechische Tragödie*. Göttingen, 1993.

Leadbeater, L. W., "In Defense of Cocteau: Another View of *La machine infernale*," *Classical and Modern Literature* 10.2 (1990), 113–125.

Lefevre, E., "Die Unfähigkeit, sich zu erkennen: Unzeitgemäße Bemerkungen zu Sophokles' *Oidipous Tyrannos*," *Würzburger Jahrbücher für die Altertumswissenschaft*, n.s. 13 (1987), 37–58.

———, *Die Unfähigkeit, sich zu erkennen: Sophokles' Tragödien*. Leiden, 2001.

Lehmann, J., "Phantastik als Schwellen- und Ambivalenzphänomen," in *Phantastik—Kult oder Kultur? Aspekte eines Phänomens in Kunst, Literatur und Film*, ed. C. Ivanovic, J. Lehrmann, and M. May. Stuttgart, 2003, 25–39.

Lesky, A., *Die tragische Dichtung der Hellenen*. Göttingen, 1972.

Lesky, A., and Herbig, R., "Sphinx," *RE* 3.A.2, col. 1717.

Lévi-Strauss, C., *Anthropologie structurale*. Paris, 1958.

Lloyd-Jones, H., and Wilson, N. G., *Sophoclea: Studies in the Text of Sophocles*. Oxford, 1990.

Lurje, M., *Die Suche nach der Schuld: Sophokles' Oedipus Rex, Aristoteles' Poetik und das Tragödienverständnis der Neuzeit*. Munich, 2004.

Lurker, M. "Hund und Wolf in ihrer Beziehung zum Tode," *Antaios* 10 (1968/1969), 199–216.

———, "Der Hund als Symboltier für den Übergang vom Diesseits in das Jenseits," *Zeitschrift für Religions- und Geistesgeschichte* 35 (1983), 132–144.

Macho, T., "Narziß und der Spiegel: Selbstrepräsentation in der Geschichte der Optik," in *Narcissus: Ein Mythos von der Antike bis zum Cyberspace*, ed. A.-B. Renger. Stuttgart, 2002, 13–25.

Margalit, A., "Meanings and Monsters," *Synthese* 44 (1980), 313–346.

Marinelli, L., ed., *"Meine . . . alten und dreckigen Götter": Aus Sigmund Freuds Sammlung*. Frankfurt am Main, 1998.

Marny, D., *Die Schönen Cocteaus: Biographie*. Hamburg, 1999.

Mason, G., "La Machine Infernale: A Modern Adaptation of the Oedipus Legend by Jean Cocteau," *Greece & Rome* 9.27 (1940), 178–187.

McDonald, M., and Walton, M., ed., "The Dramatic Legacy of Myth: Oedipus in Opera, Radio, Television and Film," in *The Cambridge Companion to Greek and Roman Theatre*. Cambridge, 2007, 303–326.

Meier, C., *Die Entstehung einer autonomen Intelligenz bei den Griechen*, in *Kulturen der Achsenzeit*, ed. S. N. Eisenstadt. Frankfurt am Main, 1987.

———, *Die politische Kunst der griechischen Tragödie*. Munich, 1988.

Mertens, W., and Haubl, R., *Der Psychoanalytiker als Archäologe*. Stuttgart, 1996.

Milorad, "La clé des mythes dans l'oeuvre de Cocteau," *Cahiers Jean Cocteau* 2 (1971), 97–140.

Moddelmog, D., *Readers and Mythic Signs: The Oedipus Myth in Twentieth-Century Fiction*. Carbondale, 1993.

Möller, D., *Jean Cocteau und Igor Strawinsky: Untersuchungen zur Ästhetik und zu "Oedipus Rex."* Hamburg, 1981.

Moret, J.-M., *OEdipe, la Sphinx et les Thebains: Essai de mythologie iconographique,* 2 vols. Rome, 1984.

Mueller, M., *Children of Oedipus and Other Essays on the Imitation of Greek Tragedy, 1550–1800.* Toronto, 1980.

Müller, C. W., "Die thebanische Trilogie des Sophokles und ihre Aufführung im Jahre 401: Zur Frühgeschichte der antiken Sophokles Rezeption und der Überlieferung des Textes," *Rheinisches Museum für Philologie* 139 (1996), 193–224.

Nilsson, M. P., "Der Oidipusmythos," *Göttingische Gelehrte Anzeigen* 184 (1922), 36–46.

O'Brien, M. J., ed., *Twentieth Century Interpretations of Oedipus Rex: A Collection of Critical Essays.* Englewood Cliffs, NJ, 1968.

Ogundele, P. A., "The Oedipus Story in the Hands of Sophocles, Seneca and Corneille," *Nigeria and the Classics* 12 (1970), 31–51.

Paduano, G., *Lunga storia di Edipo Re: Freud, Sofocle e il teatro occidentale.* Turin, 1994.

Page, H. D., "The Resurrection of the Sophoclean Phoenix: Jean Cocteau's *La machine infernale,*" *Classical and Modern Literature* 18.4 (1998), 329–343.

Papaizos, A., "Autorité mantique et autorité politique: Tirésias et Oedipe," *Kernos* 3 (1990), 307–318.

Petit, T., *Œdipe et le Cherubin: Les sphinx levantins, cypriotes et grecs comme gardiens d'Immortalité.* Fribourg, 2011.

Philp, H., *Freud and Religious Belief.* London, 1956.

Poetter, J., ed., *J. Cocteau: Gemälde, Zeichnungen, Keramik, Tapisserien, Literatur, Theater, Film, Ballett.* Cologne, 1989.

Pohle, B., *Kunstwerk Frau: Inszenierungen von Weiblichkeit in der Moderne.* Frankfurt am Main, 1998.

Pollock, G., *Psychoanalysis and the Image: Transdisciplinary Perspectives.* Malden, MA, 2006.

Pötscher, W., *Hellas und Rom.* Hildesheim, 1988.

Propp, V., "Edip v svete fol'klora," *Ucenye zapiski Leningradskogo Gosudarstvennogo Universiteta / Serija filologiceskich nauk* 9.72 (1944), 138–175 (= "Oedipus in the Light of Folklore," in *Oedipus: A Folklore Casebook,* ed. L. Edmunds and A. Dundes. New York, 1983, 76–121).

Quinn, S., *A Mind of Her Own: The Life of Karen Horney.* New York, 1987.

Racker, H., "On Freud's Position towards Religion," *American Imago* 13 (1956), 97–121.

Rainey, R., *Freud as Student of Religion: Perspectives on the Background and Development of His Thought.* Missoula, 1975.

Ransohoff, R., "Sigmund Freud: Collector of Antiquities, Student of Archaeology," *Archaeology* 28 (1975), 102–111.

Rave, K., *Orpheus bei Cocteau: Psychoanalytische Studie zu Jean Cocteaus dichterischem Selbstverständnis.* Frankfurt am Main, 1984.

Reinhard, K., "The Freudian Things: Construction and the Archaeological Metaphor," in *Excavations and Their Objects: Freud's Collection of Antiquity,* ed. S. Barker. Albany, 1996, 57–79.

Reinhardt, K., *Sophokles.* Frankfurt am Main, 1933.

Renger, A.-B., *Zwischen Märchen und Mythos: Die Abenteuer des Odysseus und andere Geschichten von Homer bis Walter Benjamin: Eine gattungstheoretische Studie*. Stuttgart, 2006.

———, "Ödipus vor der Sphinx im 5. Jahrhundert v. Chr. Einführende Bemerkungen zu einer mythischen Konstellation in Text und Bild," in Winkler-Horaček, *Wege der Sphinx* (2011), 169–178.

Ritter, N., "Die andere Sphinx—Torwächter und Schutzwesen in Assyrien," in Winkler-Horaček, *Wege der Sphinx* (2011), 67–76.

Robert, C., *Oidipus: Geschichte eines poetischen Stoffes im Altertum*, vol. 1. Berlin, 1915.

Rohde-Dachser, C., *Expedition in den dunklen Kontinent: Weiblichkeit im Diskurs der Psychoanalyse*. Berlin, 1991.

Rösler, W., *Polis und Tragödie*. Konstanz, 1980.

Roßbach, N., *Mythos Ödipus: Texte von Homer bis Pasolini*. Leipzig, 2005.

Rubins, J. L., *Karen Horney: Gentle Rebel of Psychoanalysis*. New York, 1978.

Rudnytsky, P. L., *Freud and Oedipus*. New York, 1987.

Rzach, A., "Kyklos," *RE* 11, col. 2347–2435.

Sayers, J., *Mothers of Psychoanalysis: Helene Deutsch, Karen Horney, Anna Freud, Melanie Klein*. New York, 1991.

Schade, H., *Dämonen und Monstren: Gestaltungen des Bösen in der frühen Kunst des Mittelalters*. Regensburg, 1962.

Schadewaldt, W., *Hellas und Hesperien*. Zürich, 1970.

Scharfenberg, J., *Sigmund Freud and His Critique of Religion*. Philadelphia, 1988.

Schell, M., *Marlene Dietrich: Portrait eines Mythos*. (VHS, 94 min.). Munich: Bayerischer Rundfunk, 1983.

Scherer, J., *Dramaturgies d'Œdipe*. Paris, 1987.

Schlesier, R., *Konstruktionen der Weiblichkeit bei Sigmund Freud: Zum Problem von Entmythologisierung und Remythologisierung in der psychoanalytischen Theorie*. Frankfurt am Main, 1981.

———, "Auf den Spuren von Freuds Ödipus," in *Antike Mythen in der europäischen Tradition*, ed. H. Hofmann. Tübingen, 1999, 281–300.

Schmidt, J., "Sophokles, König Ödipus: Das Scheitern des Aufklärers an der alten Religion," in *Aufklärung und Gegenaufklärung in der europäischen Literatur: Philosophie und Politik von der Antike bis zur Gegenwart*, ed. J. Schmidt. Darmstadt, 1988, 33–55.

Schmitt, A., "Menschliches Fehlen und tragisches Scheitern: Zur Handlungsmotivation im Sophokleischen 'König Ödipus,'" *Rheinisches Museum für Philologie* 131 (1988), 8–30.

Sebeok, T. A., ed., *Myth: A Symposium* (Bibliographical and Special Series of the American Folklore Society, vol. 5). Philadelphia, 1955.

Segal, C., *Oedipus Tyrannus: Tragic Heroism and the Limits of Knowledge*. New York, 1992.

Segal, H., *Melanie Klein*. New York, 1979.

Seidensticker, B., "Beziehungen zwischen den beiden Oidipusdramen des Sophokles," *Hermes* 100 (1972), 255–274.

Sigmund Freud Museum, Vienna, *Internationaler Psychoanalytischer Verlag 1919–1938* (Sigmund Freud House Bulletins), Special issue 1 (1995).

Simon, E., *Das Satyrspiel Sphinx des Aischylos*. Heidelberg, 1981.

Sophocles, *Oedipus Tyrannus*, trans. R. C. Jebb (1897). Bristol, 2011.

———, *Oedipus the King*, trans B. Knox. New York, 2005.

———, *Oedipus the King*, trans. D. Grene. Chicago, 2010.

Steinmann, U., *Die Darstellung von Mischwesen in der französischen Kultur des neunzehnten Jahrhunderts am Beispiel der Sphinx* (Diploma Thesis), Vienna, 2000.

Stephan, I., *Musen & Medusen: Mythos und Geschlecht in der Literatur des 20. Jahrhunderts*. Cologne/Weimar/Vienna, 1997.

Stockreiter, K., "Am Rand der Aufklärungsmetapher: Korrespondenzen zwischen Archäologie und Psychoanalyse," in Marinelli, *"Meine . . . alten und dreckigen Götter,"* (1998), 81–93.

Szlezák, T. A., "Ödipus nach Sophokles," in *Antike Mythen in der europäischen Tradition*, ed. H. Hofmann. Tübingen, 1999, 199–220.

Theile, W., "Stoffgeschichte und Poetik: Literarischer Vergleich von Ödipusdramen (Sophokles, Corneille, Gide)," *arcadia* 10 (1975), 34–51.

Töchterle, K., *Lucius Annaeus Seneca: Oedipus: Kommentar mit Einleitung, Text und Übersetzung*. Heidelberg, 1994.

———, "Wortgeklingel: Konstrukt oder Sprachmagie? Zum Libretto von Strawinskys *Oedipus Rex*," in *Resonanzen: Innsbrucker Beiträge zum modernen Musiktheater bei den Salzburger Festspielen*, ed. C. Mühlegger and B. Schwarzmann-Huter. Innsbruck, 1998, 113–126.

Turner, V., *The Forest of Symbols: Aspects of Ndembu Ritual*. Ithaca, 1967.

———, *The Ritual Process: Structure and Anti-Structure*. Chicago, 1969 [*Das Ritual: Struktur und Anti-Struktur*. Frankfurt am Main, 1989].

Unterburg, M., *Mythos Marlene: Die Dietrich und das 'Dritte Reich'* (VHS, 43 min.). Mainz: ZDF, 2004.

Valette, B., "Modernité du mythe chez Cocteau," *Revue de l'Université de Bruxelles* 1–2 (1989), 7–22.

van Gennep, A., *Les rites de passage* (1909) [*The Rites of Passage*, London, 1960].

Vernant, J.-P., *Les origines de la pensée grecque* (Paris, 1962) [*The Origins of Greek Thought*. Ithaca, 1982].

———, *Mythe et société en Grèce ancienne* (Paris, 1981) [*Myth and Society in Ancient Greece*. Atlantic Highlands, NJ, 1980; repr. New York, 1988].

———, *Mortals and Immortals: Collected Essays*. Princeton, NJ, 1992.

———, *Entre mythe et politique*. Paris, 1996.

Vernant, J.-P., and Vidal-Naquet, P., eds., *Mythe et tragédie en Grèce ancienne* (Paris, 1973) [*Myth and Tragedy in Ancient Greece*, trans. J. Lloyd. New York/Cambridge, 1988].

Vidal-Naquet, P., "Œdipe à Vicence et à Paris: Deux moments d'une histoire," *Quaderni di storia* 14 (1981), 3–21.

Vilsmaier, J., *Marlene: Die Legende, der Mythos, der Film* (DVD, 126 min.). Manaus: Imagem Filmes, 2000.

Vogt, R., *Psychoanalyse zwischen Mythos und Aufklärung oder das Rätsel der Sphinx*. Frankfurt am Main, 1989.

von Fritz, K., *Antike und moderne Tragödie: Neun Abhandlungen*. Berlin, 1962.

Walter, H., "Sphingen," *Antike und Abendland* 9 (1960), 60–72.

Weiß, C., and Weiß, H., "Dem Beispiel jener Forscher folgend . . . Zur Bedeutung der Archäologie im Leben Freuds," *Luzifer-Amor: Zeitschrift zur Geschichte der Psychoanalyse* 3 (1989), 45–71.

Wesolowska, E., "The Image of Oedipus in Modern Literature," *Aufidus* 40 (2000), 79–88.

Wilson, J. P., *The Hero and the City: An Interpretation of Sophocles' Oedipus at Colonus.* Ann Arbor, 1997.

Winkler-Horaček, L., "Der geflügelte Menschenlöwe (Sphinx): Ein Bildmotiv der frühgriechischen Vasenmalerei und sein Verhältnis zu den östlichen Vorbildern," in *Griechische Keramik im kulturellen Kontext: Akten des Internationalen Vasen Symposions in Kiel vom 24. bis 28.9.2001*, ed. B. Schmaltz and M. Söldner. Münster, 2003, 225–228.

———, "Sphinx im frühen Griechenland und thebanische Sphinx (Kat 30–37), in *Ägypten—Griechenland—Rom: Abwehr und Berührung*. Städelsches Kunstinstitut und Städtische Galerie, ed. H. Beck and P. Bol, Tübingen, 2005, 90–96 and 477–483.

———, "Fiktionale Grenzräume im Frühen Griechenland," in *Mensch und Tier in der Antike—Grenzziehung und Grenzüberschreitung*, ed. A. Alexandridis, M. Wild, and L. Winkler-Horaček. Wiesbaden, 2008, 493–515.

———, ed., *Wege der Sphinx: Monster zwischen Orient und Okzident*. Rahden, Westphalia, 2011.

Winter, S., *Jean Cocteaus frühe Lyrik: Poetische Praxis und poetologische Reflexion*. Berlin, 1994.

Wurnig, V., *Gestaltung und Funktion von Gefühlsdarstellungen in den Tragödien Senecas: Interpretationen zu einer Technik der dramatischen Stimmungserzeugung*. Frankfurt am Main, 1982.

Wyss, U., "Jenseits der Schwelle: Die Phantasik der anderen Welt," in *Phantastik—Kult oder Kultur? Aspekte eines Phänomens in Kunst, Literatur und Film*, ed. C. Ivanovic et al. Stuttgart, 2003, 41–53.

Yarrow, R., "Ambiguity and the Supernatural in Cocteau's *La machine infernale*," in *Staging the Impossible: The Fantastic Mode in Modern Drama*, ed. P. Murphy (London, 1992), 108–115.

Zeitlin, F. I., "Thebes: Theater of Self and Society in Athenian Drama," in *Nothing to Do with Dionysos? Athenian Drama in Its Social Context*, ed. J. J. Winkler and F. I. Zeitlin. Princeton, 1990, 130–167.

Zink, N., *Sophokles: König Ödipus*. Frankfurt am Main, 1979.

INDEX

62
88

?